ROBERT BURNS

FOOD & DRINK

12 WORKS INSPIRED BY FOOD & DRINK

ALASTAIR TURNBULL

BIG RED RESOURCES

Contents

- INTRODUCTION 1
- JOHN BARLEYCORN MUST DIE 6
- NO CHURCHMAN AM I 15
- SCOTCH DRINK 21
- ADDRESS TO A HAGGIS 37
- A BOTTLE AND FRIEND 45
- WILLIE BREW'D A PECK O MAUT 49
- TO WILLIAM STEWART 56
- THE POET'S GRACIES 61
- THE SELKIRK GRACE 66
- TAM O' SHANTER 70
- THE SHEPHERD'S WIFE 93
- O AN YE WERE DEAD GUDEMAN 101
- GLOSSARY 107
- ABOUT THE AUTHOR 169
- ALSO BY ALASTAIR TURNBULL 172

All text, except the words of Robert Burns, Copyright © 2017 by Alastair Turnbull

All rights reserved.

No part of this book may be reproduced in any form or by any electronic or mechanical means, including information storage and retrieval systems, without written permission from the author, except for the use of brief quotations in a book review.

INTRODUCTION

A Brief Introduction to Robert Burns

Robert Burns was born on the 25th of January 1759 in a small cottage in Ayrshire, the first of six sons and daughters to William and Agnes Burnes. He was born into what we would now call "abject poverty", but his family was hard working and they believed in education. Robert, along with his brothers and sisters, was taught at home by his father and a few family friends. They were tutored in the evening, after they had finished working on the farm during the day.

Robert was also lucky enough to attend the local school for a few months.

Robert grew up working hard on the land and reading avidly. He gained a great interest in poems and songs from his mother and his aunt, who were both well known for singing old Scots songs and retelling old Scottish tales. He first picked up the quill and wrote when he was just 15 years old, the subject of this poem was a girl, 'handsome Nell'. This innocent, but inspirational gesture, was the first of many great poems and songs that Robert would write in his lifetime.

Robert became a father at the age of 26, (with his mothers servant girl, Elizabeth Paton). He went on to have nine children with his wife, Jean Armour, and three other children with different women. Farming didn't provide nearly enough of an income, so early in Robert's life he accepted an offer to become a book keeper on a plantation in Jamaica. He needed money to travel and a friend suggested that he should publish his poems to fund the trip.

A printer in Kilmarnock published his book in 1786 called, "Poems Chiefly in the Scottish Dialect". It was a success and lead to him becoming the 18th century equivalent of a "local celebrity". Robert changed his mind about going to Jamaica. He received encouragement to print another, larger, edition of his works from a leading Edinburgh critic. After borrowing a pony, he travelled to Edinburgh and within two weeks had found a printer willing to publish his larger edition. This edition was also a great success. Robert sold his rights to this book to the printer, for 100 guineas, a large sum of money at the time, but this was a decision he regretted later in life.

Robert's life then became more complicated than that of a mere tenant farmer from Ayr. He mixed with the great and the good from Edinburgh society, joined drinking and debating clubs, travelled all over Scotland and was welcomed in many stately homes. This was a very enjoyable part of Robert's life, but sadly, it didn't last for ever and he eventually found himself back working on his family farm.

Later in life Robert left farming, mainly due to ill health, and the fact that it was very hard work with little reward. He became an excise man and moved to Dumfries, taking his wife and family with him. He continued to write poetry and collect songs throughout his lifetime. He is credited with writing over 500 poems and 300 songs.

Robert Burns died on the 21st July 1796.

The name of 'Robert Burns' means different things to different people. The majority will remember poems such as "My love is like a red, red rose", "Ae fond kiss" and "Tam O' Shanter". This will conjure up images of flowers, lovers, rural Scottish landscapes and mystical beings. This is the image of Scotland's "Ploughman poet", which is only one side of Robert Burns.

There are many other aspects to Robert Burns, such as Burns the Radical; he spoke out against the hypocrisy of the church and the injustice of the class system. Burns the Revolutionary; he supported the French Revolution and the American War of Independence - both of which happened during his lifetime. Burns the Scotsman; he was fiercely proud of Scotland and a Jacobite sympathiser.

The aspect of Robert Burns that we are looking at in this book, is his love of food & drink. We will look at 12 works written by Robert, and examine the food, drinks and people that inspired him. Also included are modern English translations of the poems. These translations are here purely as an aid to understanding the original poems, as the old Scots dialect Burns used, can be difficult to understand.

1
JOHN BARLEYCORN MUST DIE

Robert wrote his version of this song in 1782 at the tender age of 23. However, even in Burns time the song was already hundreds of years old.

This is the story of the harvest legend. John Barleycorn represents the spirit of Barley, grown over the summer months, cut down in his prime (harvested), then ground down and made into, bread, beer or whisky.

This harvest legend goes all the way back to ancient times. In those times John Barleycorn wasn't just the spirit of Barley he was a metaphor for the harvest cycle, and some say he was even a metaphor for life itself.

In this, Robert Burns' version, John Barleycorn is made into whisky. Each verse shows a piece of the journey from sowing the seed to harvesting, threshing, malting, milling and drinking.

Cheers!

John Barleycorn must die
By Robert Burns
Written: 1782
Type: Poem / Ballad
Tune: ?

There was three kings into the east,
    Three kings both great and high,
    And they hae sworn a solemn oath
    John Barleycorn should die.

They took a plough and plough'd him down,
    Put clods upon his head,
    And they hae sworn a solemn oath
    John Barleycorn was dead.

But the cheerful Spring came kindly on,
    And show'rs began to fall;
    John Barleycorn got up again,
    And sore surpris'd them all.

The sultry suns of Summer came,
    And he grew thick and strong;
    His head weel arm'd wi' pointed spears,
    That no one should him wrong.

The sober Autumn enter'd mild,
    When he grew wan and pale;
    His bending joints and drooping head
    Show'd he began to fail.

His colour sicken'd more and more,
    He faded into age;
    And then his enemies began
    To show their deadly rage.

They've taen a weapon, long and sharp,
    And cut him by the knee;
    Then tied him fast upon a cart,
    Like a rogue for forgerie.

They laid him down upon his back,
    And cudgell'd him full sore;
    They hung him up before the storm,
    And turned him o'er and o'er.

They filled up a darksome pit,
    With water to the brim;
    They heaved in John Barleycorn,
    There let him sink or swim.

They laid him out upon the floor,
    To work him further woe;
    And still, as signs of life appear'd,
    They toss'd him to and fro.

They wasted o'er a scorching flame,
    The marrow of his bones;
    But a miller us'd him worst of all,
    For he crush'd him between two stones.

And they hae taen his very heart's blood,
    And drank it round and round;

And still the more and more they drank,
Their joy did more abound.

John Barleycorn was a hero bold,
    Of noble enterprise;
    For if you do but taste his blood,
    'Twill make your courage rise.

'Twill make a man forget his woe;
    'Twill heighten all his joy;
    'Twill make the widow's heart to sing,
    Tho' the tear were in her eye.

Then let us toast John Barleycorn,
    Each man a glass in hand;
    And may his great posterity
    Ne'er fail in old Scotland!

John Barleycorn must die
    By Robert Burns
    Written: 1782
    Type: Poem / Ballad
    Tune:?

Modern Translation

There was three Kings into the east,
    Three Kings both great and high,
    And they have sworn a solemn oath –
    John Barleycorn should die.

They took a plough and ploughed him down,
    Put clods of earth upon his head,
    And they have sworn a solemn oath
    John Barleycorn was dead.

But the cheerful Spring came kindly on,
    And showers began to fall;
    John Barleycorn got up again,
    And completely surprised them all.

The humid suns of summer came,
    And he grew thick and strong;
    His head well armed with pointed spears,
    That no-one should him wrong.

The sober autumn entered mild,

When he grew ill and pale;
His bending joints and drooping head
Show's he's begun to fail.

His colour sickened more and more,
    He faded into age;
    And then his enemies began
    To show their deadly rage.

They have taken a weapon, long and sharp,
    And cut him by the knee;
    Then tied him securely upon a cart,
    Like a rogue for forgery.

They laid him down upon his back,
    And beat him, full sore;
    They hung him up before the storm,
    And turned him over and over.

They filled up a darksome pit,
    With water to the brim;
    They heaved in John Barleycorn,
    There let him sink or swim.

They laid him out upon the floor,
    To give him further woe;
    And still, as signs of life appeared,
    They tossed him to and fro.

They wasted, over a scorching flame,
    The marrow of his bones;
    But a Miller used him worst of all,
    For he crushed him between two stones.

And they have taken his very heart's blood,
    And drank it round and round;
    And still the more and more they drank,
    Their joy did more abound.

John Barleycorn was a hero bold,
    Of noble enterprise;
    For if you do but taste his blood,
    It will make your courage rise.

It will make a man forget his woe;
    It will heighten all his joy;
    It will make the widow's heart to sing,
    Although the tear were in her eye.

Then let us toast John Barleycorn,
>   Each man a glass in hand;
>   And may his great posterity
>   Never fail in old Scotland!

A Little Extra....

In Scotland John Barleycorn is synonymous with whisky.

The John Barleycorn legend is sometimes intertwined with the legend of 'The Green Man'. Although, 'The Green Man' is associated more with rebirth and fertility.

A version of this song is included in the 'Bannatyne Manuscript' of 1568.

2
NO CHURCHMAN AM I

Robert wrote this song in 1782, at the age of 23.

Although Robert was only 23 he had already become a freemason and had spent some time living in Irvine, trying to learn flax dressing. At the time Irvine was a major seaport. He was unsuccessful at flax dressing but was beginning to see a little more of life outside the family farm.

This is a drinking song that warns us about some of the pitfalls in life. The message this song leaves us with is a familiar one - as long as you have some friends and a bottle to share, you are not doing too badly.

No Churchman Am I
By Robert Burns

Written: 1782
Type: Song
Tune: Prepare, my dear Brethren, to the tavern let's fly

No churchman am I for to rail and to write,
    No statesman nor soldier to plot or to fight,
    No sly man of business contriving a snare,
    For a big-belly'd bottle's the whole of my care.

The peer I don't envy, I give him his bow;
    I scorn not the peasant, though ever so low;
    But a club of good fellows, like those that are here,
    And a bottle like this, are my glory and care.

Here passes the squire on his brother – his horse;
    There centum per centum, the cit with his purse;
    But see you the crown how it waves in the air?
    There a big-belly'd bottle still eases my care.

The wife of my bosom, alas! She did die;
    For sweet consolation to church I did fly;
    I found that old Solomon proved it fair,

That a big-belly'd bottle's a cure for all care.

I once was persuaded a venture to make;
    A letter inform'd me that all was to wreck;
    But the pursy old landlord just waddl'd upstairs,
    With a glorious bottle that ended my cares.

"Life's cares they are comforts" – a maxim laid down
    By the Bard, what d'ye call him, that wore the
    black gown;
    And faith I agree with th' old prig to a hair,
    For a big-belly'd bottle's a heav'n of a care.

THIS LAST STANZA WAS ADDED, (PROBABLY FROM A MASONIC LODGE)

Then fill up a bumper and make it o'erflow,
    And honours Masonic prepare for the throw;
    May ev'ry true brother of the compass and square,
    Have a big-belly'd bottle, when harass'd with
    care.

No Churchman Am I

By Robert Burns
Written: 1782
Type: Song
Tune: Prepare, my dear Brethren, to the tavern let's fly

Modern Translation

No churchman am I for to rail and to write,
    No statesman, nor soldier to plot or to fight,
    No sly man of business contriving a snare,
    For a big-bellied bottle's the whole of my care.

The peer I don't envy, I give him his bow;
    I scorn not the peasant, though ever so low;
    But a club of good fellows, like those that are here,
    And a bottle like this, are my glory and care.

Here passes the squire on his brother – his horse;
    There centum per centum, the citizen with his purse;
    But see you the crown how it waves in the air?
    There a big-bellied bottle still eases my care.

The wife of my bosom, alas! She did die;
   For sweet consolation to church I did fly;
   I found that old Solomon proved it fair,
   That a big-bellied bottle's a cure for all care.

I once was persuaded a venture to make;
   A letter informed me that all was to wreck;
   But the pursy old landlord just waddled upstairs,
   With a glorious bottle that ended my cares.

"Life's cares they are comforts" – a maxim laid down
   By the Bard, what do you call him, that wore the black gown;
   And faith I agree with the old prig to a hair,
   For a big-bellied bottle's a heaven of a care.

THIS LAST STANZA WAS ADDED, (PROBABLY FROM A MASONIC LODGE)

Then fill up a bumper and make it overflow,
   And honours Masonic prepare for the throw;
   May every true brother of the compass and

square,
Have a big-bellied bottle, when harassed with care.

A Little Extra…

A 'bumper' is a glass filled to the top with something alcoholic.

Flax Dressing is the trade of breaking and scutching Flax. This is done in preparation for spinning and dying the flax.

Robert returned to the farm penniless after the shop in which he was learning the flax dressing trade burnt to the ground. Here is an account of it in his own words:
   "*My partner was a scoundrel of the first water, who made money by the mystery of thieving; and to the whole, while we were giving a welcome carousel to the new year, our shop burnt to ashes and left me, like a true poet, not worth sixpence.*"

3
SCOTCH DRINK

This is the second poem in 'The Kilmarnock Edition', Robert's first published book of poems. He wrote it in 1785 whilst working on the family farm at Mossgiel, near Mauchline.

This poem extols the virtues of '*guid auld Scotch Drink*'. It not only celebrates whisky, but it shows us a snapshot of a simple life, with a possibility that even the poor maybe happy.

This starts with a passage from the bible, which has been translated into Scots, which talks about '*strong drink*' firing the blood, easing pain and encouraging you to have a good time. It then goes on to sing the praise's of Scotch Whisky and Scottish life until in verse 14 it warns against drinking any Brandy, '*Or foreign gill*'.

The poem finishes with what Robert thought, at the time of writing, were amongst the most important things in life; clothes to wear, food to eat, whisky to drink and words to rhyme.

Scotch Drink
>By Robert Burns
>**Written:** 1785
>**Type:** Poem

Gie him strong drink until he wink,
>That's sinking in despair;
>An' liquor guid to fire his bluid,
>That's prest wi' grief and care:
>There let him bouse, an deep carouse,
>Wi' bumpers flowing o'er
>Till he forgets his loves or debts,
>An' minds his griefs no more.
>*Solomon's Proverbs, xxxi. 6 – 7*

Let other poets raise a fracas
>'Bout vines, an' wines, an' drucken Bacchus,
>An' crabbit names an' stories wrack us,
>An' grate our lug:
>I sing the juice Scotch bear can mak us,

In glass or jug.

O thou, my muse!guid auld Scotch drink!
    Whether thro' wimpling worms thou jink,
    Or, richly brown, ream owre the brink,
    In glorious faem,
    Inspire me, till I lisp an' wink,
    To sing thy name!

Let husky wheat the haughs adorn,
    An' aits set up their awnie horn,
    An' pease and beans, at e'en or morn,
    Perfume the plain:
    Leeze me on thee, John Barleycorn,
    Thou King o' grain!

On thee aft Scotland chows her cood,
    In suople scones, the wale o' food!
    Or tumbling in the boiling flood
    Wi Kail an' beef;
    But when thou pours thy strong heart's blood,
    There thou shines chief.

Food fills the wame, an' keeps us leevin;

Tho' life's a gift no worth receivin,
When heavy-dragged wi' pine an' grievin;
But oil'd by thee,
The wheels o' life gae down-hill, scrievin,
Wi rattlin glee.

Thou clears the head o'doited Lear;
Thou cheers ahe heart o' drooping care;
Thou strings the nerves o' Labour sair,
At's weary toil;
Though even brightens dark Despair
Wi' gloomy smile.

Aft, clad in massy siller weed,
Wi' gentles thou erects thy head;
Yet, humbly kind in time o' need,
The poor man's wine;
His weepdrap parritch, or his bread,
Thou kitchens fine.

Thou art the life o' public haunts;
But thee, what were our fairs and rants?
Ev'n godly meetings o' the saunts,
By thee inspired,
When gaping they besiege the tents,

Are doubly fir'd.

That merry night we get the corn in,
    O sweetly, then, thou reams the horn in!
    Or reekin on a New-year morning
    In cog or bicker,
    An' just a wee drap sp'ritual burn in,
    An' gusty sucker!

When Vulcan gies his bellows breath,
    An' ploughmen gather wi' their graith,
    O rare! To see the fizz an freath
    I' ht' luggit caup!
    Then Burnewin comes on like death
    At every chap.

Nae mercy then, for airn or steel;
    The brawnie, banie, ploughman chiel,
    Brings hard owrehip, wi sturdy wheel,
    The strong forehammer,
    Till block an' studdie ring an reel,
    Wi' dinsome clamour.

When skirling weanies see the light,

Though maks the gossips clatter bright,
How fumblin' cuiffs their dearies slight;
Wae worth the name!
Nae howdie gets a social night,
Or plack frae them.

When neibors anger at a plea,
An' just as wud as wud can be,
How easy can the barley brie
Cement the quarrel!
It's aye the cheapest lawyer's fee,
To taste the barrel.

Alake! That e'er my muse has reason,
To wyte her countrymen wi' treason!
But mony daily weet their weason
Wi' liquors nice,
An' hardly, in a winter season,
E'er Spier her price.

Wae worth that brandy, burnin trash!
Fell source o' mony a pain an' brash!
Twins mony a poor, doylt, drucken hash,
O' half his days;
An' sends, beside, auld Scotland's cash

To her warst faes.

Ye Scots, wha wish auld Scotland well!
    Ye chief, to you my tale I tell,
    Poor, packless devil's like mysel'!
    It sets you ill,
    Wi' bitter, dearthfu' wines to mell,
    Or foreign gill.

May gravels round his blather wrench,
    An' gouts torment him, inch by inch,
    What twists his gruntle wi' a glunch
    O' sour disdain,
    Out owre a glass o' whisky-punch
    Wi' honest men!

O' whisky! Soul o' plays and pranks!
    Accept a bardie's gratfu' thanks!
    When wanting thee, what tuneless cranks
    Are my poor verses!
    Thou comes-they rattle in their ranks,
    At ither's a-s!

Thee, Ferintosh! O sadly lost!

Scotland lament frae coast to coast!
Now colic grips, an' barkin hoast
May kill us a';
For loyal Forbes' charter'd boast
Is ta'en awa?

Thae curst horse-leeches o' the Excise,
    Wha mak the whisky stells their prize!
    Haud up thy han', Deil! Ance, twice, thrice!
    There, seize the blinkers!
    An' bake them up in brunstane pies
    For poor damn'd drinkers.

Fortune! If thou'll but gie me still
    Hale breeks, a scone, an' whisky gill,
    An' rowth o' rhyme to rave at will,
    Tak a' the rest,
    An' deal't about as thy blind skill
    Directs thee best.

Scotch Drink
    By Robert Burns
    Written: 1785
    Type: Poem

Modern Translation

Give him strong drink until he wink,
    That is sinking in despair;
    And liquor good to fire his blood,
    That is pressed with grief and care.
    There let him drink deeply, and deep carouse,
    With bumpers flowing over,
    Till he forgets his loves or debts,
    And minds his grieves no more.
Solomon's Proverbs, xxxi. 6, 7

Let other poets raise a fracas
    About vines, and wines, and drunken Bacchus,
    And ill-natured names and stories torment us,
    And annoy our ear;
    I sing the juice Scotch Barley can make us,
    In glass or jug.

O you, my muse! Good old Scotch drink!
    Whether through winding worms you leap,
    Or, richly brown, cream over the brink,
    In glorious foam,
    Inspire me, till I lisp and wink,
    To sing your name!

Let husky wheat the hollows adorn,
    And oats set up their bearded horn,
    And peas and beans, at evening or morning,
    Perfume the plain;
    Blessings on you, John Barleycorn,
    You King of grain!

On you often Scotland chews her cud,
    In supple scones, the pick of food!
    Or tumbling in the boiling soup,
    With vegetables and beef;
    But when you pour your strong heart's blood,
    There you shine chief.

Food fills the belly, and keeps us living,
    Although life is a gift not worth receiving,
    When heavy dragged with pine and grieving;
    But oiled by you,
    The wheels of life go downhill, careering,
    With rattling glee.

You clear the head of muddled learning,
    You cheer the heart of drooping care;

You string the nerves of Labour sore,
At its weary toil;
You even brighten dark despair
With a gloomy smile.

Often clad in a massif silver dress,
   With gentles you erect your head;
   Yet, humbly kind in time of need,
   The poor man's wine;
   His little drop of porridge, or his bread,
   You make good food.

You are the life of public haunts,
   Without you what were our friars and
   merry makings?
   Even godly meetings of the saints,
   By you inspired,
   When, gaping, they besiege the tents,
   Are doubly fired.

That merry night we get the corn in,
   O sweetly, then, you take the spoon in!
   Or smoking on a New Year morning
   In dish or beaker,
   And just a small drop spiritual burn in,

    And tasty sugar!

When Vulcan gives his bellows breath,
    And ploughmen gather with their wealth,
    O rare! To see you fizz and froth
    In the two-eared cup!
    Then the blacksmith comes on like death
    At every stroke.

No mercy, then, for iron or steel;
    The brawny, bony, ploughman fellow,
    Brings hard overhip, with sturdy wheel,
    The strong forehammer,
    Till block and anvil ring and reel,
    With noisy clamour.

When squalling babies see the light,
    You make the gossips babble cheerfully;
    How fumbling dolts their darlings slight;
    Woe befall the name!
    No midwife gets a social night,
    Or coin from them.

When neighbours anger at a law case,

And just as wild as wild can be,
How easy can the barley brew
Cement the quarrel!
It is always the cheapest lawyer's fee,
To taste the barrel.

Alas! That ever my Muse has reason,
　To charge her countrymen with treason!
　But many daily wet their throat
　With liquors nice,
　And hardly, in a winter season,
　Ever asks her price.

Woe befall that brandy, burning trash!
　Fierce source of many a pain and illness!
　Robs many a poor, stupid, drunken oaf,
　Of half his days;
　And sends, beside, old Scotland's cash
　To her worst foes.

You Scots, who wish old Scotland well!
　You chief, to you my tale I tell,
　Poor, penniless devils like myself!
　It makes you ill,
　With bitter, scarce wines to meddle,

Or foreign gill.

May small stones round his bladder wrench,
    And gouts torment him, inch by inch,
    Who twists his face with a growl
    Of sour disdain,
    Out over a glass of whisky-punch
    With honest men!

O Whisky! Soul of plays and pranks!
    Accept a Bards grateful thanks!
    When wanting thee, what tuneless creaking's
    Are my poor verses!
    You come, they rattle in their ranks
    At others arses!

You Ferintosh! O sadly lost!
    Scotland's lament from coast to coast!
    Now colic grips, and barking cough
    May kill us all;
    For loyal Forbes chartered boast
    Is taken away.

Those cursed horse leeches of the Excise,

Who make the whisky stills their prize!
Hold up your hand, Devil, once, twice, three times!
There seize the spies!
And bake them up in brimstone pies
For poor damned drinkers.

Fortune! If you will but give me still
    Whole trousers, a scone, and whisky gill,
    And a store of rhyme to rave at will,
    Take all the rest,
    And deal it about as your blind skill
    Directs you best.

A Little Extra…

'Bacchus' is the Greek God of wine.

In verse 18 '*Ferintosh*' and '*Loyal Forbes*' are mentioned. Ferintosh is a town on the Black Isle, northwest Scotland, and was part of the Forbes Estate. The Forbes family had given loyal service to the Covenanters and the Marquis of Argyll but their property and possessions suffered in the conflict. As compensation the crown granted them the right to distil whisky and be excused excise duty. Within a hundred years Ferintosh was selling more whisky than all the other parts of Scotland put together. In 1784 the crown bought back the right to excise duty for the princely sum of £22,500.

Robert Burns was a big fan of a fellow poet called '*Robert Fergusson*'. Fergusson's poem 'Caller Water' may well have influenced Burns when writing ''Scotch Drink'.

4
ADDRESS TO A HAGGIS

This is one of Robert's most famous and regularly performed poems. It is a fundamental part of any 'Burns Supper' and usually recited by the host or a special guest.

This address / poem was officially written in 1786 not long after Robert arrived in Edinburgh. It is said that he wrote it for a dinner party that was being held at his friend Andrew Bruce's house. However, it is possible that Robert had been using a version of this poem before he arrived in Edinburgh. It is rumored that Robert composed the last stanza extempore at a dinner in the home of John Morrison, a cabinet-maker from Mauchline. One thing we can be sure of is that the poem first appeared in the 'Caledonian Mercury' on the 19th of December 1786 and in the 'Scots Magazine' in January 1787. This was the first Burns poem to be printed in any periodical, (newspaper /magazine).

This is one of the few pieces of note that Robert produced in this period. This was probably due to the fact that he was enjoying being introduced to Edinburgh Society, meeting new people and generally having as good a time as possible.

In the poem itself Robert presents the haggis as a unique and symbolic part of Scottish culture. He tells us that haggis tastes great and is good for you. He then goes on to warn against eating more elegant, foreign foods and looking down on haggis as being inferior.

Address To A Haggis
By Robert Burns
Written: 1786
Type: Address

Fair fa' your honest, sonsie face,
    Great chieftain o' the pudding-race!
    Aboon them a' yet tak your place,
    Painch, tripe, or thairm:
    Weel are ye wordy o' a grace

As lang's my arm.

The groaning trencher there ye fill,
    Your hurdies like a distant hill,
    Your pin was help to mend a mill
    In time o'need,
    While thro' your pores the dews distil
    Like amber bead.

His knife see rustic Labour dight,
    An' cut you up wi' ready sleight,
    Trenching your gushing entrails bright,
    Like ony ditch;
    And then, O what a glorious sight,
    Warm-reekin', rich!

Then, horn for horn, they stretch an' strive:
    Deol tak the hindmost! On they drive,
    Till a' their weel-swall'd kytes believe
    Are bent like drums;
    Then auld Guidman, mast like to rive,
    Bethankit! Hums.

Is there that owre his French ragout

    Or olio that wad staw a sow,
    Or fricassee wad make her spew
    Wi' perfect sconner,
    Looks down wi' sneering, scornfu' view
    On sic a dinner?

Poor devil! See him owre his trash,
    As feckles as withr'd rash,
    Hi spindle shank, a guid whip-lash;
    His nieve a nit;
    Thro' blody flood or field to dash,
    O how unfit!

But mark the Rustic, haggis-fed,
    The trembling earth resounds his tread.
    Clap in his walie nieve a blade,
    He'll mak it whissle;
    An' legs an' arms, an' hands will sned,
    Like taps o' trissle.

Ye pow'rs wha mak mankind your care,
    And dish them out their bill o'fare,
    Auld Scotland wants nae skinking ware
    That jaups in luggies;
    But if ye wish her gratefu' prayer

Gie her a haggis!

Address To A Haggis
By Robert Burns
Written: 1786
Type: Address

Modern Translation

Good luck to you and your honest, plump face,
    Great chieftain of the sausage race!
    Above them all you take your place,
    Stomach, tripe, or intestines!
    Well are you worthy of a grace
    As long as my arm.

The groaning trencher there you fill,
    Your buttocks like a distant hill,
    Your pin would help to mend a mill -
    In time of need,
    While through your pores the dews distil,
    Like amber bead.

His knife see rustic Labour wipe,
    And cut you up with ready slight,
    Trenching your gushing entrails bright,
    Like any ditch;
    And then, O what a glorious sight,
    Warm steaming, rich!

Then spoon for spoon, they stretch and strive,
    Devil take the hindmost, on they drive,
    Till all their well swollen bellies by and by
    Are bent like drums;
    Then the old head of the table,
    most likely to burst,
    'The Grace!' hums.

Is there that over his French ragout,
    Or olio that would sicken a sow,
    Or fricassee would make her vomit –
    With perfect disgust,
    Looks down with sneering, scornful view
    On such a dinner?

Poor devil! See him over his trash,
    As feeble as a withered rush,
    His thin legs a good whip-lash,

His fist a nut;
Through bloody flood or field to dash –
O' how unfit!

But mark the rustic, haggis-fed,
The trembling earth resounds his tread,
Held in his ample fist a blade,
He'll make it whistle;
And legs and arms, and heads will cut off,
Like the heads of thistles.

You powers, who make mankind your care,
And dish them out their bill of fare,
Old Scotland wants no watery stuff,
That splashes in small wooden bowls;
But if you wish her grateful prayer,
Give her a Haggis!

A Little Extra …..

Haggis was traditionally made from 'sheep's pluck', i.e. heart, liver and lungs, minced with onion, oatmeal, suet, some spices and salt. This was then mixed with stock and encased in the sheep's stomach. It was cooked by boiling it in water.

The first known (written) recipe for haggis appeared in 'Cookery and Pastry' by Susanna Maciver, 1787. It is however a traditional dish and was in use long before then.

In Burns' day, haggis was not an everyday meal, in fact, it could have been described as a 'luxury item'.

Modern day haggis hasn't changed that much from it historical predecessor. The main difference is that the haggis is encased in a sausage skin, not the sheep's stomach. There are also new variations, such as vegetarian haggis.

This poem was probably influenced by Robert Fergusson's poem 'Caller Oysters'. It was also written in the standard 'Habbie' stanza, which Burns made his own.

5
A BOTTLE AND FRIEND

This was written by Robert in 1787. It is basically a short song that encourages good cheer, friendship and social drinking.

This song may only consist of two short verses but it contains some great lines and deep thought. The line, *"Then catch the moments as they fly, and use them as you ought man"*, is very similar to 'Carpe Diem' but pre-dates it by over 200 years.

This song is telling us to enjoy what we have, even if it's just a few drinks with some friends – because you don't know what is around the next corner…

A Bottle And Friend
　By Robert Burns
　Written: 1787

Type: Song
Tune: ?

Here's a bottle and an honest friend!
    What wad ye wish for mair, man?
    Wha kens, before his life may end,
    What his share may be o' care, man?

Chorus
    There's nane that's blest of human kind,
    But the cheerful and the gay, man,
    Fal, la, la, etc…

Then catch the moments as they fly,
    And use them as ye ought, man:
    Believe me, happiness is shy,
    And comes not aye when sought, man.

Chorus
    There's nane that's blest of human kind,
    But the cheerful and the gay, man,
    Fal, la, la, etc…

A Bottle And Friend
By Robert Burns
Written: 1787
Type: Song
Tune: ?

Modern Translation

Here's a bottle and an honest friend!
What would you wish for more, man?
Who knows, before his life may end,
What his share may be of care, man?

Chorus
There's none that's blessed of human kind,
But the cheerful and the happy, man,
Fal, la, la etc…

Then catch the moments as they fly,
And use them as you ought, man:
Believe me, happiness is shy,
And comes not always when sought, man.

Chorus
>There's none that's blessed of human kind,
>But the cheerful and the happy, man,
>Fal, la, la etc…

A Little Extra …

This song could be looked upon as being quite sadly autobiographical for Robert. He did indeed enjoy what he had, but suffered more than his fair share of hardship.

In 1787 Robert published his second edition of poems, known as the 'Edinburgh Edition'.

6
WILLIE BREW'D A PECK O MAUT

One of life's great pleasures is getting together with friends and enjoying each other's company. Talking, laughing, drinking and having a good time is a great way to spend your free time. Robert, like most of us, also loved good company and a good night out.

One day in August / September 1789 he went to the town of Moffat, which is in the Scottish Borders, with his friend Allan Masterton. They went to visit another friend, William Nicol, at lodgings he had taken there. It turns out that the three of them had a really good time. They were drinking, singing, talking and joking for most of the night. At some point in the evening inspiration must have struck them as they wrote this song. Robert wrote the lyrics, Allan wrote the music. I'm not sure what Willie did but I'm sure he had some input!

Willie Brew'd A Peck O' Maut
By Robert Burns
Written: 1789
Type: Song
Tune:?

O Willie brew'd a peck o' maut,
    And Rob and Allen cam to see;
    Three blyther hearts, that lee-lang night,
    Ye wadna found in Christendie.

Chorus
    We are na fou, we're nae that fou,
    But just a drappie in our ee;
    The cock may craw, the day may daw
    And aye we'll taste the barley bree.

Here are we met, three merry boys,
    Three merry boys I trow are we;
    And mony a night we've merry been,
    And mony mae we hope to be!

Chorus
    We are na fou, we're nae that fou,

But just a drappie in our ee;
The cock may craw, the day may daw
And aye we'll taste the barley bree.

It is the moon, I ken her horn,
    That's blinkin' in the lift sae hie;
    She shines sae bright to wyle us hame,
    But by my sooth, she'll wait a wee!

Chorus
    We are na fou, we're nae that fou,
    But just a drappie in our ee;
    The cock may craw, the day may daw
    And aye we'll taste the barley bree.

Wha first shall rise to gang awa,
    A cuckold, coward loun is he!
    Wha first beside his chair shall fa',
    He is the king amang us three.

Chorus
    We are na fou, we're nae that fou,
    But just a drappie in our ee;
    The cock may craw, the day may daw

And aye we'll taste the barley bree.

Willie Brew'd A Peck O' Maut
By Robert Burns
Written: 1789
Type: Song
Tune:?

Modern Translation

Oh, Willie brewed a pack of malt,
And Rob and Allan came to taste.
Three happier hearts that live-long night -
You would not find in Christendom.

Chorus
We are not drunk; we are not that drunk,
But just a sparkle in our eye!
The cock may crow, the day may dawn,
And always we'll taste the barley-brew!

Here are we met, three merry boys,
Three merry boys, I believe are we;

And many a night we have merry been,
And many may we hope to be!

Chorus
We are not drunk; we are not that drunk,
But just a sparkle in our eye!
The cock may crow, the day may dawn,
And always we'll taste the barley-brew!

It is the moon, I know her horn,
That is twinkling in the sky so high;
She shines so bright to encourage us home,
But, by my truth, she will wait a little!

Chorus
We are not drunk; we are not that drunk,
But just a sparkle in our eye!
The cock may crow, the day may dawn,
And always we'll taste the barley-brew!

Who first to rise to go away,
A cuckold, coward rouge is he!
Who first beside his chair shall fall,
He is the king among us three!

Chorus
>We are not drunk; we are not that drunk,
>But just a sparkle in our eye!
>The cock may crow, the day may dawn,
>And always we'll taste the barley-brew!

A Little Extra …

The lodgings they stayed in were not in the actual town of Moffat, they were close by, somewhere between Moffat and the head of the Loch of the Lowes.

A '*cuckold*' is a man who has an adulterous wife. It is also a derogatory term for someone who is sexually inadequate.

Willie Nicol also accompanied Robert on his tour of the Highlands. This took place between the 25th August and the 16th September 1787.

Allan Masterton wrote the music for a few other of Burns' songs, such as:

Strathallan's Lament
  The Braes o' Ballochmyle
  The Bonnie Birks o' Ayr
  On hearing a young lady sing
  Ye gallants bright, I rede ye right -
  (This is also known as '*Beware o' Bonnie Ann*')

'*Bonnie Ann*' is Allan Masterson's daughter. Robert wrote the song as a favor to Allan.

7
TO WILLIAM STEWART

At some point in most people's lives they fall into the trap of drinking too much and suffering from a hangover. Robert Burns was no exception.

This poem was enclosed in a letter written to his friend, William Stewart, in 1789. Robert wrote it as he sat at a table by the fire in the 'Brownhill Inn', which is a few miles north of the Burns family farm at Ellisland. It was a Monday and he had a severe hangover after enjoying a very heavy nights drinking the evening before.

This poem is all about Robert's remorse at drinking too much. He then pours out his suffering and agony as he deals with the hangover from hell.

To William Stewart

By Robert Burns
Written: 1789
Type: Poem

In honest Bacon's ingle-neuk,
    Here maun I sit and think;
    Sick o' the warld and warld's fock,
    And sick, damned sick o' drink!

I see, I see there is nae help,
    But still down I maun sink;
    Till some day, laigh enough, I yelp,
    Wae worth that cursed drink!

Yestreen alas! I was sae fu',
    I could but yisk and wink;
    And now, this day, sair, sair I rue,
    The weary, weary drink.

Satan, I fear thy sooty claws,
    I hate thy brunstane stink,
    And ay I curse the luckless cause,
    The wicked soup o' drink.

In vain I would forget my woes
   In idle rhyming clink,
   For past redemption dam'd in Prose
   I can do nought but drink.

For you, my trusty, well-try'd friend,
   May Heaven still on you blink;
   And may your life flow to the end,
   Sweet as a dry man's drink!

To William Stewart
   By Robert Burns
   Written: 1789
   Type: Poem

Modern Translation

In honest Bacon's fire-side,
   Here must I sit and think;
   Sick of the world and the world's people,
   And sick, damned sick of drink!

I see, I see there is no help,

But still down I must sink;
Till some day, low enough I cry,
Alas that cursed drink.

Last night alas! I was so drunk
    I could but hiccup and wink;
    And now this day, sore, sore I regret
    The weary, weary drink.

Satan, I fear your sooty claws,
    I hate your brimstone stink,
    And always I curse the luckless cause,
    The wicked soup of drink.

In vain I would forget my woes
    In idle rhyming jingle,
    For past redemption damned in Prose,
    I can do nothing but drink.

To you my trusty, well tried friend,
    May heaven still on you smile,
    And may your life flow to the end,
    Sweet as a dry man's drink!

A Little Extra ….

'*Honest Bacon*' is actually John Bacon, the owner of the Brownhill Inn. Mr Bacon is also the husband of Catherine Stewart, William Stewart's sister.

William Stewart, 1749 – 1812, was the son of a publican in Closeburn and a very good friend of Robert Burns. He was also the father of 'Lovely Polly Stewart'.

As well as writing the song '*Lovely Polly Stewart*' about William's daughter, Robert also wrote the song '*You're welcome Willie Stewart*'. He used his diamond tipped stylus and cut the lyrics onto a crystal tumbler in William's house. Sir Walter Scott later bought the tumbler - it is now kept at Abbotsford House.

8
THE POET'S GRACIES

These graces, one for before a meal and one for after, are thought to have been written by Robert in 1789. They were originally known as 'A Grace before Dinner' and 'A Grace after Meat'. They appeared in the 'Caledonian Mercury' on the 27th of August 1789.

It is believed, but unfortunately cannot be proved, that Robert composed and delivered these graces extempore at a dinner in Dumfries.

Neither grace was included in Robert's 'Edinburgh Edition' and they gradually fell out of use. They were rediscovered in Dr James Currie's biography in 1800. It is only in relatively recent times that they have been re-attributed to Burns and become known as 'The Poet's Graces'.

The Poets Graces
    By Robert Burns
    Written: 1789
    Type: Grace

A Grace Before Dinner

O thou who kindly dost provide
    For every creature's want!
    We bless thee, God of Nature wide,
    For all thy goodness lent:
    And if it please Thee, Heavenly Guide,
    May never worse be sent;
    Whether granted, or denied,
    Lord, bless us with content.
    Amen!

A Grace After Dinner

O thou, in whom we live and move,
    Who made the sea and shore;
    Thy goodness constantly we prove,
    And grateful would adore;
    And if it please thee, power above!

Still grant us, with such store,
The friend we trust, the fair we love,
And we desire no more.
Amen!

The Poets Graces
By Robert Burns
Written: 1789
Type: Grace

Modern Translation

A Grace Before Dinner

O Lord, who kindly dose provide
For every creature's want!
We bless you, God of Nature wide,
For all thy goodness lent:
And if it please you, Heavenly Guide,
May never worse be sent;
Whether granted, or denied,
Lord, bless us with content.
Amen!

A Grace After Dinner

O Lord, in whom we live and move,
    Who made the sea and shore;
    Your goodness constantly we prove,
    And grateful would adore;
    And if it please you, power above!
    Still grant us, with such store,
    The friend we trust, the fair we love,
    And we desire no more.
    Amen!

A Little Extra ….

Robert is well known for composing extempore, or 'off the cuff' graces. One such occasion was when Robert and a few friends arrived unexpectedly at the Globe Tavern in Dumfries, and there was no food prepared for them. The Landlord, William '*Jock*' Hyslop and his wife '*Meg*' agreed to give them the food that they had prepared for themselves, a ram's head and feet. Robert wrote the following graces for them:

Before The Meal

Oh Lord, when hunger pinches sore,
Do thou stand us in stead,
And send us, from thy bounteous store,
A tup or wether head!
Amen

After The Meal

O Lord, since we have feasted thus,
Which we so little merit,
Let Meg now take away the flesh,
And Jock bring in the spirit!

Tup - ram (male sheep)

Wether - sheep (female)

9
THE SELKIRK GRACE

Don't let the length of this small, four line grace, fool you - it is by far the most popular grace in Scotland. This grace is still said, not only at Burns suppers and events, but also regularly at family gatherings, weddings, parties, etc. It is Scotland's 'go to' grace.

Did Robert Burns write it?

The answer to that question is, unfortunately, no. Robert didn't write the Selkirk Grace. It is however, confusingly, known as Robert's most famous grace. The answer to that riddle lies in the fact that it was one of his favourite graces, and one he often used at social gatherings. The more he used the grace, the more it became associated with his name.

At the time Robert was using this grace, it was already quite old. It was known as the 'Galloway Grace', or the 'Covenanters Grace' and was said in 'Lallans' (the lowland Scots dialect). This is **version (1)** of the Selkirk Grace.

Although Robert knew the traditional grace, he did not use the 'Lallans' dialect. He preferred to recite his own version; this is **version (2),** of the Selkirk Grace.

Version (3) is a modern translation.

The Selkirk Grace (1)
Traditional (Lallans - Lowland Scots dialect)
Some hae meat and canna eat,
And some wad eat that want it,
But we hae meat and we can eat,
Sae let the Lord be thankit.

The Selkirk Grace (2)
Burns Version
Some have meat and cannot eat,
Some cannot eat that want it;
But we have meat and we can eat,

Sae let the Lord be thankit.

The Selkirk Grace (3)
　Modern Translation
　Some have meat and cannot eat,
　Some cannot eat that want it;
　But we have meat and we can eat,
　So to the Lord we give thanks.

A Little Extra …

This grace is not named after the town of Selkirk (located in the Scottish Borders) but is named after a man, Dunbar Douglas – the fourth Earl of Selkirk. Robert used it at a meal in July 1794. The meal took place at the 'Heid Inn', which is on Kirkcudbright High Street, in the presence of Lord Selkirk. This is probably when people started referring to it as 'The Selkirk Grace'.

The Inn is still there today, but is now called 'The Selkirk Arms'.

Although Robert himself used **version (2)**, people today still tend to recite the original Lallans version, **version (1)**.

10
TAM O' SHANTER

This is one of Robert's most famous poems, and it's said that of all his works, this was his favourite.

Robert wrote this poem for Frances Grose, who was at the time looking for interesting places to include in volume two of his book, '*The Antiquities of Scotland*'. During a conversation Robert had with Frances, he asked him to include a picture of Alloway Kirk. Frances agreed, as long as Robert would give him something to print beside it.

Robert wrote to Frances in June 1790 and enclosed three different stories associated with Alloway Kirk. The second story was the basis of 'Tam O' Shanter'. It was an old folk tale he had heard as a boy, probably told by his mother or aunt (Betty Davidson), about an Ayrshire farmer who liked to stay late drinking on market days and always got into trouble on the way home. Robert used this local legend as his starting point, and from there he crafted the story that we know and love today.

This story has a lot in it! It has humor, horror, social comment, drinking, colorful characters and dancing witches. However, this is a cautionary tale, remember Tam O' Shanters mare…

Tam O' Shanter
By Robert Burns
Written: 1790
Type: A Tale

When chapman billies leave the street,
    And drouthy neibors, neibors meet;
    As market days are wearing late,
    And folk began to tak the gate,
    While we sit bousing at the nappy,
    An' getting fou and unco happy,
    We think na on the lang Scots miles,
    The mosses, waters, slaps and stiles,
    That lie between us and our hame,
    Where sits our sulky, sullen dame,
    Gathering her brows like a gathering storm,

Nursing her wrath to keep it warm.

This truth fand honest Tam o' Shanter,
    As he frae Ayr ae night did canter:
    Auld Ayr, wham ne'er a town surpasses,
    For honest men and bonie lasses.

O Tam! Had'st thou but been sae wise,
    As taen thy ain wife Kate's advice!
    She tauld thee weel thou was a skellum,
    A blethering, blustering, drunken blellum;
    That frae November till October,
    Ae market-day thou was na sober;
    That ilka melder wi' the Miller,
    Thou sat as lang as thou had siller;
    That ev'ry naig was ca'd a shoe on
    The Smith and thee gat roarin' fou on;
    That at the Lord's house, ev'n on Sunday,
    Thou drank wi' Kirkton Jean till Monday,
    She prophesied that late or soon,
    Thou wad be found, deep drown'd in Doon,
    Or catch'd wi' warlocks in the mirk,
    By Alloway's auld, haunted kirk.

Ah, gentle dames! It gars me greet,

To think how mony counsels sweet,
How mony lengthen'd, sage advices,
The husband frae the wife despises!

But to our tale: Ae market night,
    Tam had got planted unco right,
    Fast by an ingle, bleezing finely,
    Wi reaming swats, that drank divinely;
    And at his elbow, Souter Johnie,
    His ancient, trusty, drouthie crony:
    Tam lo'ed him like a very brither;
    They had been fou for weeks the gither.
    The night drave on wi' sangs an' clatter;
    And aye the ale was growing better:
    The Landlady and Tam grew gracious,
    Wi' favours secret, sweet, precious:
    The Souter tauld his queerest stories;
    The Landlords laugh was ready chorus:
    The storm without might rair and rustle,
    Tam did na mind the storm a whistle.

Care, mad to see a man sae happy,
    E'en drown'd himself amang the nappy.
    As bees flee hame wi' lades o' treasure,
    The minutes wing'd their way wi' pleasure:
    Kings may be blest, but Tam was glorious,

O'er a' the ills o' life victorious!

But pleasures are like poppies spread,
    You seize the flow'r, its bloom is shed;
    Or like the snow falls in the river,
    A moment white – then melts forever;
    Or like the Borealis race,
    That flit ere you can point their place;
    Or like the rainbow's lovely form
    Evanishing amid the storm.
    Nae man can tether Time nor Tide,
    The hour approaches Tam maun ride;
    That hour, o' night's black arch the key-stane,
    That dreary hour he mounts his beast in;
    And sic a night he taks the road in,
    As ne'er poor sinner was abroad in.

The wind blew as 'twad blawn its last;
    The rattling showers rose on the blast;
    The speedy gleams the darkness swallow'd;
    Loud, deep and lang, the thunder bellow'd:
    That night, a child might understand,
    The deil had business on his hand.

Weel-mounted on his grey mare, Meg,

A better never lifted leg,
Tam skelpit on thro' dub and mire,
Despising wind, and rain, and fire;
Whiles holding fast his gude blue bonnet,
Whiles crooning o'er some auld Scots sonnet,
Whiles glow'rin round wi' prudent cares,
Lest bogles catch him unawares;
Kirk-Alloway was drawing nigh,
Where ghaists and houlets nightly cry.

By this time he was cross the ford,
    Where in the snaw the chapman smoor'd;
    And past the birks and meikle stane,
    Where drunken Charlie brak's neck-bane;
    And thro' the whins, and by the cairn,
    Where hunters fand the murder'd bairn;
    And near the thorn, aboon the well,
    Where Mungo's mither hang'd hersel'.
Before him doon pours all his floods,
The doubling storm roars thro' the woods,
The lightnings flash from pole to pole,
Near and more near the thunders roll,
When glimmering thro' the groaning trees,
Kirk-Alloway seem'd in a bleeze,
Thro' ilka bore the beams were glancing,
And loud resounded mirth and dancing.

Inspiring bold John Barleycorn!
    What dangers thou canst make us scorn!
    Wi' tippenny, we fear nae evil;
    Wi' usquabae, we'll face the devil!
    The swats sae ream'd in Tammie's noddle,
    Fair play, he car'd na deils a boddle,
    But Maggie stood, right sair astonish'd,
    Till, by the heel and hand admonish'd,
    She ventur'd forward on the light;
    And wow! Tam saw an unco sight!

Warlocks and witches in a dance:
    Nae cotillion, brent new frae France,
    But hornpipes, jigs, strathspeys, and reels,
    Put life and mettle in their heels.
    A winnock-bunker in the east,
    There sat auld Nick, in shape o' beast;
    A towzie tyke, black, grim, and large,
    To gie them music was his charge:
    He screw'd the pipes and gart them skirl,
    Till roof and rafters a' did dirl,
    Coffins stood round, like open presses,
    That shaw'd the dead in their last dresses;
    And (by some devilish cantraip sleight)
    Each in its cauld hand held a light.
    By which heroic Tam was able
    To note upon the haly table,

A murderer's banes, in gibbet-airns;
Twa span-lang, wee, unchristened bairns;
A thief, new-cutted frae a rape,
Wi' his last gasp his gabudid gape;
Five tomahawks, wi' blude red-rusted:
Five scimitars, wi' murder crusted;
A garter which a babe had strangled:
A knife, a father's throat had mangled.
Whom his ain son of life bereft,
The grey-hairs yet stack to the heft;
Wi' mair of horrible and awfu',
Which even to name wad be unlawfu'.
Three lawyers tongues, turned inside oot,
Wi' lies, seamed like a beggars clout,
Three priests hearts, rotten, black as muck,
Lay stinkin, vile in every nuke.

As Tammie glowr'd, amaz'd, and curious,
   The mirth and fun grew fast and furious;
   The piper loud and louder blew,
   The dancers quick and quicker flew,
   They reel'd, they set, they cross'd, they cleekit,
   Till ilka carlin swat and reekit,
   And coost her duddies to the wark,
   And linkit at it in her sark!

Now Tam, O Tam! Had they been queans,
>   A' plump and strapping in their teens!
>   Their sarks, instead o' creeshie flainen,
>   Been snaw-white seventeen hunder linen!
>   Thir breeks o' mine, my only pair,
>   That ance were plush o' guid blue hair,
>   I wad hae gien them off my hurdies,
>   For a blink o' the bonie burdies!
>   But wither'd bedlams, auld and droll,
>   Rigwoodie hags wad spean a foal,
>   Louping an flinging on a crummock.
>   I wonder did na turn thy stomach.

But Tam kent what was what fu' brawlie:
>   There was ae winsome wench and waulie,
>   That night enlisted in the core,
>   Lang after ken'd on Carrick shore;
>   (For mony a beast to dead she shot,
>   And perish'd mony a bonie boat,
>   And shook baith meikle corn and bear,
>   And kept the country-side in fear);
>   Her cutty sark, o'Paisley harn,
>   That while a lassie she had worn,
>   In longitude tho' sorely scanty,
>   It was her best, and she was vauntie.
>   Ah! Little ken'd thy reverend grannie,
>   That sark she coft for her wee Nannie,

Wi' twa pund Scots('twas a' her riches),
Wad ever grac'd a dance of witches!

But here my Muse her wing maun cour,
    Sic flights are far beyond her power;
    To sing how Nannie lap and flang,
    (A souple jade she was and strang),
    And how Tam stood, like ane bewitch'd,
    And thought his very een enrich'd:
    Even Satan glowr'd, and fidg'd fu' fain,
    And hotch'd and blew wi' might and main:
    Till first ae caper, syne anither,
    Tam tint his reason a' the-gither,
    And roars out, "Weel done, Cutty-Sark!"
    And in an instant all was dark:
    And scarcely had he Maggie rallied.
    When out the hellish legion sallied.

As bees bizz out wi' angry fyke,
    When plundering herds assail the byke;
    As open pussie's mortal foes,
    When, pop! She starts before their nose;
    As eager runs the market-crowd,
    When "Catch the thief!" resounds aloud;
    So Maggie runs, the witches follow,
    Wi' mony an eldritch skreich and hollow.

Ah, Tam! Ah, Tam! Thou'll get thy fairin!
    In hell, they'll roast thee like a herrin!
    In vain thy Kate awaits thy comin!
    Kate soon will be a woefu' woman!
    Now, do thy speedy-utmost, Meg,
    And win the key-stone o' the brig;
    There, at them thou thy tail may toss,
    A running stream they dare na cross.
    But ere the keystone she could make,
    The fient a tail she had to shake!
    For Nannie, far before the rest,
    Hard upon noble Maggie prest,
    And flew at Tam wi' furious ettle;
    But little wist she Maggie's mettle!
    Ae spring brought off her master hale,
    But left behind her ain grey tail:
    The carlin claught her by the rump,
    And left poor Maggie scarce a stump.

Now, wha this tale o' truth shall read,
    Ilk man and mother's son, take heed:
    Whene'er to Drink you are inclin'd
    Or Cutty-sarks rin in your mind,
    Think ye may buy the joys o'er dear;
    Remember Tam o' Shanter's mare.

Tam O' Shanter
>By Robert Burns
>**Written:** 1790
>**Type:** A Tale

Modern Translation

When peddler people leave the street,
>And thirsty neighbours, neighbours meet;
>As market days are wearing late,
>And folk began to take the road home,
>While we sit boozing strong ale,
>And getting drunk and very happy,
>We don't think of the long Scots miles,
>The marshes, waters, steps and stiles,
>That lye between us, and our home,
>Where sits our sulky, sullen wife,
>Gathering her brows like a gathering storm,
>Nursing her wrath to keep it warm.

This truth finds Tam o' Shanter,
>As he from Ayr one night did canter:
>Old Ayr, which never a town surpasses,

For honest men and bonny lasses.

O Tam! Had you but been so wise,
    As to have taken your own wife Kate's advice!
    She told you well, you were a rogue,
    A rambling, blustering, drunken boaster;
    That from November untill October,
    Each market-day you were never sober;
    That each milling period, with the Miller,
    You sat as long as you had money;
    That every horse he put a shoe on,
    The blacksmith and you got roaring drunk on;
    That at the Lord's house, even on Sunday,
    You drank with Kirkton Jean till Monday,
    She prophesied that late or soon,
    you would be found, deep drowned in Doon,
    Or caught by warlocks in the murk,
    By Alloway's auld, haunted church.

Ah, gentle ladies! It makes me cry,
    To think how many counsels sweet,
    How many long, wise advices,
    The husband from the wife despises!

But to our tale: One market night,

Tam was seated just right,
Next to a fireplace, blazing finely,
With excellent ales, that drank divinely;
And at his elbow, Cobbler Johnny,
His old, trusty, thirsty friend:
Tam loved him like a very brother;
They had been drunk for weeks together.
The night drove on with songs and chatter;
And every ale was growing better:
The Landlady, and Tam, grew gracious,
With secret favours, sweet and precious:
The Cobbler told his strangest stories;
The Landlords laugh was ready chorus:
Outside, the storm might roar and rustle,
Tam did not mind the storm a whistle.

Care, mad to see a man so happy,
    Even drowned himself in good ale.
    As bees fly home with lots of treasure,
    The minutes winged their way with pleasure:
    Kings may be blessed, but Tam was glorious,
    Over all the ills of life victorious!

But pleasures are like poppies spread,
    You seize the flower, its bloom is shed;
    Or like the snow falls in the river,

A moment white – then melts forever;
Or like the Aurora Borealis rays,
That jump before you can point their place;
Or like the rainbow's lovely form
Vanishing amid the storm.
No man can tether Time or Tide,
The hour approaches, Tam must ride;
That hour, of night's black arch the key-stone,
That dreary hour he mounts his horse in;
And such a night he takes the road in,
As never a poor sinner has been out in.

The wind blew as if it had blown its last;
    The rattling showers rose on the blast;
    What little light the darkness swallowed;
    Loud, deep and long, the thunder bellowed:
    That night, a child might understand,
    The devil had business on his hand.

Well-mounted on his grey mare, Meg,
    A better never lifted a leg,
    Tam raced on through mud and mire,
    Despising wind, and rain, and fire;
    While holding fast his good blue bonnet,
    While singing over some old Scots sonnet,
    Whilst glowering round with prudent cares,

Incase ghosts catch him unawares;
Alloway's church was drawing near,
Where ghosts and owels, nightly cry.

By this time he was across the ford,
    Where in the snow the peddler got smothered;
    And past the birch trees and large stone,
    Where drunken Charlie broke neck-bone;
    And through the thorns, on past the cairn,
    Where hunters found the murdered child;
    And near the thorn, above the well,
    Where Mungo's mother hanged herself.
    Before him, the river Doon, pours all his floods,
    The doubling storm roars through the woods,
    The lightning flashes from pole to pole,
    Near and more near the thunders roll,
    When - shining through the groaning trees,
    Kirk-Alloway seemed in a blaze,
    Through every gap,
    the beams of light were glancing,
    And loud resounded mirth and dancing.

Inspiring, bold, whisky!
    What dangers you can make us forget!
    With ale, we fear no evil;
    With whisky, we'll face the devil!

The ales so swam in Tam's head,
Fair play, he didn't care at all for Devils,
But Maggie stood, completely astonished,
Till, by the heel and hand led on,
She ventured forward on the light;
And wow! Tam saw an unbelievable sight!

Warlocks and witches in a dance:
    No cotillion, (dances), brand-new from France,
    But hornpipes, jigs, strathspeys, and reels,
    Put life and mettle in their heels.
    In a window alcove in the east,
    There sat old Nick, in the shape of a beast;
    A shaggy dog, black, grim, and large,
    To give them music was his charge:
    He screwed the bagpipes and made them squeal,
    Till roof and rafters all did ring,
    Coffins stood round, like open presses,
    That showed the dead in their last dresses;
    And by some devilish magic sleight
    Each in its cold hand held a light.
    By which heroic Tam was able
    To note upon the holy table,
    A murderer's bones, in an iron cage;
    Two span-long, small, unchristened children;
    A thief, newly cut, from his hanging rope,
    With his last gasp his mouth gaped open;

Five tomahawks, with blood, red-rusted:
Five scimitars, with murder crusted;
A garter with which a baby was strangled:
A knife, a father's throat had mangled.
Whom his own son, of life deprived,
The grey-hairs yet stuck to the shaft;
With more of horrible and awful,
Which even to name would be unlawful.
Three lawyers tongues, turned inside out,
Sewn with lies, like a beggars cloth,
Three priests hearts, rotten, black as muck,
Lay stinking, vile in every corner.

As Tam looked on, amazed, and curious,
    The mirth and fun grew fast and furious;
    The piper loud and louder blew,
    The dancers quick and quicker flew,
    They reeled, they set, they crossed, they linked,
    Till every witch sweated and stank,
    And cast their dirty clothes to the floor,
    And danced heartily in their underskirts!

Now Tam, O Tam! Had they been younger girls,
    All plump and strapping in their teens!
    Their underskirts, instead of greasy flannel,
    Been snow-white seventeen hundred linen!

These trousers of mine, my only pair,
That once were plush of good blue hair,
I would have given them off my buttocks,
For a blink of the pretty women !

But withered hags, old and droll,
    Ugly enough to suckle a foal,
    Leaping an flinging on a bent stick.
    Its a wonder it didn't turn your stomach.

But Tam knew what was well enough:
    There was one winsome happy wench,
    That night enlisted in the core,
    Long after known on Carrick shore;
    (For many a beast to dead she shot,
    And perished many a bonnie boat,
    And shook both lots of corn and barley,
    And kept the country-side in fear);
    Her short underskirt, of Paisley cloth,
    That while a young girl, she had worn,
    In length though, not nearly enough,
    It was her best, and she was proud.
    Ah! Little knew, your reverend grandmother,
    That underskirt she bought
    for her little granddaughter,
    With two Scots pounds, (it was all her riches),

Would ever have graced a dance of witches!

But here my tale must stoop and bow,
    Such words are far beyond her power;
    To sing how Nannie leaped and kicked,
    (A supple youth she was and strong),
    And how Tam stood, like one bewitched,
    And thought his very eye's enriched:
    Even Satan glowered, and fidgeted full of lust,
    And thrust and blew with might and main:
    Till first one caper, then another,
    Tam lost his reason all together,
    And roars out, "Well done, short underskirt!"
    And in an instant all was dark:
    And scarcely had he Maggie rallied.
    When out the hellish legion sallied.

As bees buzz out with angry wrath,
    When plundering herds attack the hive;
    As a wild hare's mortal foes,
    When, pop! She starts running before their nose;
    As eager runs the market-crowd,
    When "Catch the thief!" resounds aloud;
    So Maggie runs, the witches follow,
    With many an unearthly scream and shout.

Ah, Tam! Ah, Tam! you'll get what's coming!
    In hell, they'll roast you like a herring!
    In vain your Kate awaits your coming!
    Kate soon will be a sad, sad woman!
    Now, do your speedy utmost, Meg,
    And beat them to the key-stone of the bridge;
    There, at them, you may toss your tail,
    A running stream they dare not cross.
    But, before the keystone she could make,
    At the fiend, a tail she had to shake!
    For Nannie, far before the rest,
    Hard upon noble Maggie pressed,
    And flew at Tam with furious intension;
    But little knew she of Maggie's mettle!
    One spring, delivered her master, whole,
    But left behind her own grey tail:
    The witch caught her by the rump,
    And left poor Maggie scarce a stump.

Now, to whom this tale of truth shall read,
    Each man and mother's son, take heed:
    Whenever to Drink you are inclined
    Or short underskirts run in your mind,
    Think! You may buy the joys over dear;
    Remember Tam o' Shanter's mare.

A Little Extra ….

This poem was first published in the '*Edinburgh Magazine*' in March 1791. It was also published one month later in the Francis Grose book 'The *Antiquities of Scotland*', volume two.

According to the Scottish writer 'John Gibson Lockhart' Robert wrote this poem in a single day.

The Ayrshire legend that inspired '*Tam O' Shanter*' may well have been based on a real person, Douglas Graham of Shanter Farm, Carrick. He supplied his cousin's inn with barley. Unfortunately he often sat in the inn with his good friend, John Davidson, and drank the money he had made from the sale of the barley. It is believed that one night, on his way home, he lost his bonnet, in the lining of which was the day's takings from the market. To cover up this loss, he told his wife that he had seen witches in the Kirk, and that they had chased him. He told her that he only just got away over the stream, but had lost his bonnet, and his horses tail, in the process.

A 'Tam O' Shanter' is the name given to a flat crowned woollen hat with a pom-pom.

11
THE SHEPHERD'S WIFE

Robert wrote this rustic tale of married life in 1792. It's not completely original, but based on a traditional song passed down from generation to generation by word of mouth.

This song is basically a conversation between a wife and her husband. The wife is at home and is shouting to her husband who is a shepherd working up in the hills, asking him to come home. She tries to entice him home by telling him what food she has prepared - but it is another offer that eventually brings him home…

The Shepherd's Wife
    By Robert Burns
    Written: 1792
    Type: Song
    Tune: ?

Chorus

    The Shepherd's wife cries o'er the knowe,
    "Will ye come hame, will ye come hame ?"
    The Shepherd's wife cries o'er the knowe,
    "Will ye come hame, again e'en jo ?"
    "O what will ye gie me to my supper,
    Gin I come hame, gin I come hame,
    O what will ye gie me to my supper,
    Gin I come hame again e'en jo ?"

"Ye'se get a panfu' o' plumpin parridge,
    And butter in them, and butter in them,
    "Ye'se get a panfu' o' plumpin parridge,
    Gin ye'll come hame, again e'en jo ?"
    " Ha ha, how ! that's naethin that dow,
    I winna come hame, I canna come hame;
    Ha, ha, how ! that's naethin that dow,
    I winna come hame gin e'en jo".

Chorus

    The Shepherd's wife cries o'er the knowe,
    "Will ye come hame, will ye come hame ?"
    The Shepherd's wife cries o'er the knowe,
    "Will ye come hame, again e'en jo ?"

"O what will ye gie me to my supper,
Gin I come hame, gin I come hame,
O what will ye gie me to my supper,
Gin I come hame again e'en jo ?"

"A reekin fat hen, weel fryth'd i' the pan,
   Gin ye'll come hame, gin ye'll come hame,
   A reekin fat hen, weel fryth'd i' the pan,
   Gin ye'll come hame again e'en jo ?"
   " Ha ha, how ! that's naethin that dow,
   I winna come hame, I canna come hame;
   Ha, ha, how ! that's naethin that dow,
   I winna come hame gin e'en jo".

Chorus
   The Shepherd's wife cries o'er the knowe,
   "Will ye come hame, will ye come hame ?"
   The Shepherd's wife cries o'er the knowe,
   "Will ye come hame, again e'en jo ?"
   "O what will ye gie me to my supper,
   Gin I come hame, gin I come hame,
   O what will ye gie me to my supper,
   Gin I come hame again e'en jo ?"

"A weel made bed and a pair o' cleen sheets,

Gin ye'll come hame, gin ye'll come hame,
A weel made bed and a pair o' clean sheets,
Gin ye'll come hame again e'en Jo ?"
" Ha ha, how ! that's naethin that dow,
I winna come hame, I canna come hame;
Ha, ha, how ! that's naethin that dow,
I winna come hame gin e'en jo".

Chorus
The Shepherd's wife cries o'er the knowe,
"Will ye come hame, will ye come hame ?"
The Shepherd's wife cries o'er the knowe,
"Will ye come hame, again e'en jo ?"
"O what will ye gie me to my supper,
Gin I come hame, gin I come hame,
O what will ye gie me to my supper,
Gin I come hame again e'en jo ?"

"A luvin wife in lilly-white linens,
Gin ye'll come hame, gin ye'll come hame,
A luvin wife in lilly-white linens,
Gin ye'll come hame again e'en jo ?"
"Ha, ha, how ! that's something that dow,
I will come hame, I will come hame;
Ha, ha, how ! that's something that dow,
I will come hame again e'en jo".

The Shepherd's Wife
By Robert Burns
Written: 1792
Type: Song
Tune: ?

Modern Translation

Chorus

The shepherd's wife cries over the hill,
"Will you come home, will you come home?"
The shepherd's wife cries over the hill,
"Will you come home by evening my love?"
"Oh what will you give me, for my supper,
If I come home, if I come home,
Oh what will you give me for my supper,
If I come home by evening my love?"

"You'll get a pan full of plumping porridge,
And butter in them, and butter in them,
You'll get a pan full of plumping porridge,
If you come home by evening my love."
"Ha, ha, how! That's nothing that able,

I will not come home; I cannot come home;
Ha, ha, how ! That's nothing that able,
I will not come home before evening my love."

Chorus

The shepherd's wife cries over the hill,
"Will you come home, will you come home?"
The shepherd's wife cries over the hill,
"Will you come home by evening my love?"
"Oh what will you give me, for my supper,
If I come home, if I come home,
Oh what will you give me for my supper,
If I come home by evening my love?"

"A smoking fat hen, well fried in the pan,
If you will come home, if you will come home,
A smoking fat hen, well fried in the pan,
If you will come home by evening my love."
"Ha, ha, how! That's nothing that able,
I will not come home; I cannot come home;
Ha, ha, how ! That's nothing that able,
I will not come home before evening my love."

Chorus

The shepherd's wife cries over the hill,

"Will you come home, will you come home?"
The shepherd's wife cries over the hill,
"Will you come home by evening my love?"
"Oh what will you give me, for my supper,
If I come home, if I come home,
Oh what will you give me for my supper,
If I come home by evening my love?"

"A well made bed and a pair of clean sheets,
    If you will come home, if you will come home,
    A well made bed and a pair of clean sheets,
    If you will come home before evening my love."
"Ha, ha, how! That's nothing that able,
I will not come home; I cannot come home;
Ha, ha, how! That's nothing that able,
I will not come home before evening my love."

Chorus
    The shepherd's wife cries over the hill,
    "Will you come home, will you come home?"
    The shepherd's wife cries over the hill,
    "Will you come home by evening my love?"
    "Oh what will you give me, for my supper,
    If I come home, if I come home,
    Oh what will you give me for my supper,
    If I come home by evening my love?"

"A loving wife in lily-white linens,
    If you come home, if you come home,
    A loving wife in lily-white linens,
    If you will come home by evening my love."
"Ha, ha, how! That's something that able,
    I will come home, I will come home;
    Ha, ha, how! That's something that able,
    I will come home before evening my love."

A Little Extra ….

In 1792 Robert was working as an excise officer in Dumfries. He also became a father again when his wife, Jean Armour, gave birth to their daughter, Elizabeth Riddell Burns.

At this time Robert was collecting a lot of songs for inclusion in James Johnson's book '*The Scots Musical Museum*'.

12
O AN YE WERE DEAD GUDEMAN

Robert wrote this song in 1795 / 1796. Once again it is his version of a traditional song, which has been passed from generation to generation by word of mouth. In his version he has altered the opening lyrics and added a more content to the verses.

This song is about a wife who wants rid of her husband, and intends to show him this by short-changing his meals.

Robert added the '*cuckold's horns*' motif to humiliate the husband, 'Gudeman'. A '*cuckold*' is a husband who has an adulterous wife. The wife saying that she wants to give her widowhood to a '*rantin highlandman'* highlights this humiliation even more.

O an ye were dead Gudeman

By Robert Burns
Written: 1795 / 1796
Type: Song
Tune: ?

Chorus
> O an ye were dead gudeman,
> A green turf on your head, gudeman,
> I wad bestow my widowhood
> Upon a rantin Highlandman.

There's sax eggs in the pan, gudeman,
> There's sax eggs in the pan, gudeman,
> There's ane to you, and twa to me,
> And three to our John Highlandman.

Chorus
> O an ye were dead gudeman,
> A green turf on your head, gudeman,
> I wad bestow my widowhood
> Upon a rantin Highlandman.

A sheep-head's in the pot, gudeman,
> A sheep-head's in the pot, gudeman;

The flesh to him the broo to me,
And the horns become your brow, gudeman.

Chorus
O an ye were dead gudeman,
A green turf on your head, gudeman,
I wad bestow my widowhood
Upon a rantin Highlandman.

Sing round about the fire wi' a rung she ran,
An rownd about the fire wi' a rung she ran;
Your horns shall tie you to the staw,
And I shall bang your hide, gudeman.

Chorus
O an ye were dead gudeman,
A green turf on your head, gudeman,
I wad bestow my widowhood
Upon a rantin Highlandman.

O an ye were dead Gudeman
By Robert Burns
Written: 1795 / 1796
Type: Song

Tune: ?

Modern Translation

Chorus
    Oh I wish you were dead good-man,
    A green turf on your head, good-man,
    I would give my widowhood
    To a roaring Highland-man.

There's six eggs in the pan, good-man,
    There's six eggs in the pan, good-man,
    There's one to you, and two to me,
    And three to our John Highland-man.

Chorus
    Oh I wish you were dead good-man,
    A green turf on your head, good-man,
    I would give my widowhood
    To a roaring Highland-man.

A sheep-head's in the pot, good-man,
    A sheep-head's in the pot, good-man;

The flesh to him, the broth to me,
And the horns become your worry, good-man.

Chorus
Oh I wish you were dead good-man,
A green turf on your head, good-man,
I would give my widowhood
To a roaring Highland-man.

Sing round about the fire, with a weapon she ran,
And around about the fire, with a weapon she ran;
Your horns shall tie you to the stall,
And I shall bang your hide, good-man.

Chorus
Oh I wish you were dead good-man,
A green turf on your head, good-man,
I would give my widowhood
To a roaring Highland-man.

A Little Extra…

This song was written / revised near to the end of Robert's life. Although he was very ill he continued to collect and amend old Scottish songs for inclusion in James Johnson's book, '*The Scots Musical Museum*'.

Robert is credited with writing and collecting a total of 368 songs.

GLOSSARY

One of the biggest barriers to understanding Burns poetry is the old and unusual Scottish dialect he often used. Although, to be fair, he was born over 250 years ago…

This glossary of Scottish words and their modern English translation should help you to break down the language barrier.

A

a' - all
albeit - although
abeigh - at a distance
aboon - above
abide - endure
abread - abrod, in sight
abreed - in breadth
a-bodie - someone
awbodie - everyone
acquent - acquainted
acqueesh - between

a'day - all day long
adle - putrid water
ado - to do
ae - one
aff - off
aff -loof - off hand
afiel - afield
afore - before
aft - often
aften - often
agee - on the side
agley - wrong / askew
ahin - behind
aiblins - perhaps
aik - oak
aiker - acre
ail - ill
ain - own
air - early
airless - money
airn - iron, iron tool
airt - direction
aith - oath
aits - oats
aisle - hot cinder
akwart - awkward
alake - alas

alane - alone
alang - along
alas - sadly
amaist - almost
amang - among
ambrie - cupboard
an - if
an' - and
ance - once
ane - one
ane - own (their)
aneath - beneath
anent - concerning
anes - ones
aneugh - enough
anither - another
ardour - passion
a's - all is
ase - ash
ashet - serving dish
asklent - squint
aspar - spread out
assail - disturb / trouble / attack
aster - stirring
atains - at once
athart - athwart (contradictory)
athole - hawk

at tour - moreover
atweel - of course
aught - possession
aughteen - eighteen
aughtlins - in any way
auld - old
auld reekie - Edinburgh (old smoky)
auld-warld - old-world
aumous - alms, (money or food given to the poor)
aumous-dish - begging bowl
ava - at all
avaunt - Go Away !
awa - away
awald - doubled up
awauk - awake
awe - owe
awfu' - awful
awnie - bearded
awsome - frightful
ayont - beyond
ay - always

B

ba' - ball
babie - baby
babie clouts - baby clothes
backet - bucket

backit - backed
backlins - backwards
bade - asked
baggie - belly
baig'nets - bayonets
baillie - magistrate
bainie - bony
bairn - child / baby
baith - both
bakes- biscuits
ballats - ballads
balloch - mountain pass
bamboozle - confound, trick
ban - curse
ban' - bond
bane - bone
bang - effort
bannet - bonnet
bannock - round flat loaf, cake
barket - barked
barley-bree - whisky
barm - yeast
bartie - the devil
batts - colic
bauchles - old shoes
bauckie-bird - a bat, (flying bat)
baudrons - cat

bauk - rafter
bauld - bold
bawbee - halfpenny
bawk - untiled ridge
baws'nt - white
bawtie - dog
bear / bere - barley
bearded-bere - ripe barley
beas' - vermin
beastie - small animal
beb - drink
bedeen - immediately
beet - fan
beets - boots
befa' - befall
beft - beaten
begrutten - in tears
beik - bask
belang - belong
beld - bald
bellum - assault
bellys - bellows
belyve - quickly / at once
ben - mountain
ben - into, through, within
benison - blessing
bent - field

bere / bear - barley
bestead - provided
bethankit - Give God thanks, grace after a meal
beuk - book
beyont - beyond
bi - by / beside
bi crivens - Christ defend us
bicker (noun) - wooden dish
bicker (verb) - stagger
bickering - argumentative
bide - stay / endure
bield - shelter
bien - prosperous
big - build
biggin - cottage
biggit - built
bill - bull
billie - friend / companion
bing - heap
birk - birch
birken-shaw - small wood
birkie - fellow
birl - carouse
birnie - rough
birr - energy
birses - bristles
bit - place

bizz - bustle
black-bonnet - church elder
blastie - mischievous
blate - bashful
blather - bladder
blathrie - chatter
blatter - rattle
blaud - large quantity
blaw - blow, exaggerate
blawart - bluebell
blest - blessed
blellum - boaster
bleezing - blazing / warming
blirt - weep / cry
blythe - gentle / kind
blythely - happily / merrily
bocked - vomited
bogle - demon / small monster
bogshaivle - distort
bonie - beautiful
bony - beautiful
boreas - the north wind
bosom - chest / breasts
bousing - boozing / drinking
bow-hough'd - bandy-legged
brachens - ferns
brae - slope, hillside

braid - broad
braid-claith - broad cloth
braird - first sprouting of corn / barley – etc
braik - harrow
braindg't - reeled
brainge - barge
brak - break
brander - gridiron (a frame of parallel bars)
brands - calf muscles
brang - bought
brankan - prancing
branks - halter (a strap or rope around the head of an animal)
brankie - gaudy / smart
brash - illness
brats - scraps
brattle - scamper / run
brattle - chatter / talk
braw - beautiful / handsome
brawlie - heartily
braxie - dead sheep
breastie - breast
breastit - sprang / jumped
brechame - halter
breckan - fern
bree - juice, (whisky)
breeks - britches / trousers

brent - smooth, high
brent -new- brand-new
brig - bridge
briss - press
brither - brother
brock - badger
brogue - trick / fool
broo - broth
brose - oatmeal dish
browden - fond / like
brownie - spirit
browst - ale / beer
brugh - burgh
brulzie - brawl / fight
brunstane - brimstone
brunt - burned
brust - burst
buff - thump
bught - pen
bughtin-time - milking-time
buirdly - stoutly
buller - bubble
bumbazed - confused
bum - clock- beetle
bummin - humming
bummle - useless person
bung - fuddled / confused

bunker - window-seat
burdie - bird / girl
bure - bore
burn - stream / brook
burnewin - blacksmith
burnie - small stream / small burn (stream)
burr-thrissle - thistle
busk - dress
buskie - bushy
buskit - dressed
buss - bush
bussle - bustle
but an' ben - kitchen & parlour
butching - butchering
byke - hive / nest

C

ca' - call
cadger - hawker
caddie - carrier / bearer
caff - chaff
cairn - pile of stones
cairts - playing cards
calf-ward - calf-pen, (enclosure)
callant - a youth (boy)
caller - bracing / cold
callet - girlfriend

cangle - wrangle
cankert - ill tempered
canna - cannot
cannie - cautious / go easy
cannie - gentle
cantie - jolly / happy
cantraip - magic spell
cape-stane - coping stone
careerin' - rushing
care na - care not
carfuffle - disorder / argument
cark - anxious
carle - old man
carline - old woman
cartes - playing cards
castock - cabbage stem
caudron - cauldron
cauf - calf
cauk - chalk
cauld - cold
cavie - coop (hen)
causey - causeway / street
ceilidh - dance / gathering
chafts - chops
chancy - fortune
change-house - ale-house / pub
chantan - chanting

chanters - bagpipes
chap (noun) - liquid measure
chap (verb) - rap / knock
chapman - pedlar
chaup - stroke
cheek-for-chow – cheek-by-jowl
chiel - fellow / man
chimla - fireplace
chimla-lug - fireside
chirm - sing
chittering - shivering
chuck - dear
chuffie - fat-faced
cit - citizen
clachan - village (small)
claes - clothes
claith - cloth
clank (ie) - knock
clarty / clartie - dirty
clash - chatter
clashmaclavers - gossip
claught - seized
claut - clean
claver - clover
clavers - tales / stories
cleed - clothe
cleek - clutch

cleekit - linked arms
cleuch - ravine
clink - coin / money
clinkin - jerking
clinkumbell - bell-ringer
clinty - stony
clips - shears
clash-ma-claver – nonsense
cloot - hoof
clout - patch
cluds - clouds
coft - bought
cog - wooden cup
commaun - command
coman - coming
comely - pleasing
cood - cud
coof - idiot / fool
cookit - hid
coor - cover
cooser - stallion
coost - cast
corbie - crow
core - crowd
corn't - fed with oats
cotter - cottage-dweller (someone who lives in a cottage)

coulter - plough blade
couthie - aggreeable / pleasant
covert - hiding place / conceal
cowe - scare / frighten
cowpit - stumbled
cow'rin - cowering
cowslip - yellow flowers
cozie - comfortable / warm
crabbit - miserable / negative
crack - conversation
craft - croft
craig - rock
craigie - throat
crambo-jingle - rhymes
cranks - creaking
cranreuch - hoar-frost / frost
crap - crop
craw - crow
creel - basket / confusion
creeshie - greasy
cronie - friend
croon - hum
crouchie - hunchbacked
crouse - merry
crowdie - porridge
crowl - crawl
crummie - cow

crummock - crooked staff
crump - crisp
cry - tell
culzie - flatter
cuif - idiot / fool
cun - earn
curch - kerchief
curmurring - commotion
curn - parcel
curple - buttocks
cutled - courted
cutty - short

D

dab - peck / pierce
daez't - bewildered
daffin - merriment
dail - plank
daidlin - waddling
daimen-icker - occasional ear of corn
dam - pent up water
dams - game of draughts
damn'd haet - damn all
dang - pushed / knocked
darg - work
darger - casual laborer
darklin - dark

daud - pelt
daunder - stroll / walk
daunton - subdue
daur - dare
daurt - dared
daut - fondle / pet
daver - wander aimlessly
dawd - lump
dawt - caress
dawin - dawning
dearthfu' - expensive
deave - deafen
defac'd - defaced
Deil - Devil
deleerit - delirious
delvin - digging
deray - disorder
dern - hidden
descrive - describe
deuk - duck
deval - descend
diddle - move quickly
differ - quarrel / dispute
dight - wipe / clean
dimpling - undulating
dink - trim
dinmont - two year old sheep

dinna - don't
dint - affection
dirk - short dagger
dizzen - dozen
docht - dared
dochter - daughter
doit - small copper coin
doited - muddled
donsie - self important
doo - dove
dool - sorrow
douce - prudent / grave
douk - duck
doup - backside
dou / doo - dove
douk - dip / bathe
dour - sullen / unhappy
dow - can / able
dowff - dismal
downa - cannot
doxy - lover / suitor
doylt - stupid
doytin - doddering
draigl't - draggled / unkempt
drants - long prayers
drap - drop
draunting - drawling

dree - suffer
dreeping - dripping
dreigh - tedious
drest - dressed
driddle - saunter / walk slow
drod - prick
droddum - backside / bum
droukit - drenched / soaked
drouth - thirst
drouthie - thirsty
drucken - drunken
drum - hillock / ridge
drumlie - muddy
drummock - oatmeal & water
drunt - bad mood
dub - puddle
duddies - ragged old clothes
dunt - hit / strike a blow
durk - dirk / short dagger
dusht - pushed / thrown
dwaum - swoon / feint
dyke - wall / dry stone wall
dynie - tremble
dyvor - Bankrupt

E
ear' - early

eard - earth
eastlin - eastern
e'ebrie - eyebrow
e'e - eye
een - eyes
e'en - even
e'enin - evening
eenou - immediately
eerie - strange / frightening
efface - erase
eggle - urge on
eke - also
eild - old age
elbuck - elbow
eldritch - unearthly
elekit - elected
eller - church elder
embower - surround / shelter
en' - end
eneugh - enough
enow - enough
erselins - backwards
esthler - carved stone
etter - fester
ettercap - spider
ettle - aim
even'd - compare

evermair - evermore
evite - shun
expeckit - expected
eydent - diligent

F

fa' - fall / to get / lot
fab - trick
faddom - fathom
fae - from / foe / enemy
faem - foam
faiket - let off / excused
fail - turf
fain - affectionate / fond
fair-fa' - welcome / good luck
fairin - present / reward
fairly - certainly
fairmers - farmers
fait - neat
faize - annoy / upset
fan - found
fand - found (past tense)
fank - sheep pen / rope coil
fankle - tangle
fantoush - flashy
farden - farthing
farl - scone / small oatcake

fash - trouble / irritate
fasht - troubled / bothered
Fasten-ee'ne - Shrove Tuesday
fat - what
fatt'rills - ribbons
fauld - fold
faun - fallen
faur - far
faur back - long ago
fause - false
faut - fault
fawsont - seemly
feal - field
fear't - frightened
fecht - fight
feck - majority / the bulk
fecket - waistcoat
feckless - weak
fcerie - sturdy
feide - fued
feil - many
feirrie - lusty
fell - deadly
felly - relentless
fent - garment opening
ferlie - wonder / marvel
fernyer - last year

fetter - bind / chain
fettle - condition
fey - fated
fickle - changeable
fidgin-fain - restless
fiel - comfortable
fient - devilish
fier - well / friend
filial - dutiful
findy - substantial
fissle - tingle
fit - foot
flacht - handful
flait / flate - scolded
flawgaires - whimsies
fleesh - fleece
fleg - frighten
flesher - butcher
fletherin - flattering
fley'd - frightened
flichtering - fluttering
flinders - shreds
flinty - hard
fliskit - fretted
flit - move
fluther - hurry
flyte - scold

fodgel - plump
foggage - a second growth of grass
fon - fond
Foorsday - Thursday
for a' that - not withstanding
foraye - forever
Forfairn - worn out
forfouchen - exhausted
forgather - meet
forker - earwig
forleet - forsake
fou - drunk / full
foughten - troubled
fouth - plenty
frae - from
frammle - gobble
frist - trust
fu' - drunk / full
fud - backside (short tail)
fushion - vigour / spirit
fusionless - spiritless / weak
fustit - decayed
fyke - fidget
fyled - soiled / fouled

G

gab - talk / mouth

gae - go
gadsman - ploughboy
gallants - splendid men
gan - begun
gane - gone
gang - go
gangrel - vagrant
gar - make
gars - makes
gash - respectable
gat - got
gate - road
gath'rin - gathering
gaud - went
gauger - exciseman
gaun - going
gawky - akward
gawsie - jolly / buxom
gear - belongings
gentie - graceful
genty - trim / elegent
get - child / offspring
ghaist - ghost
gie - give
gif - if
gilpey - young woman
gin - against

girn - grin
girnal - meal chest
grin - snarl
glaikit - foolish
glaum'd - snatched
glen - valley
gloaming - twilight
glunch - frown
gowan - daisy
gowd - gold
gowden - golden
gowdie - head
gowdspink - goldfinch
gracefu' - graceful
graff - grave
graith - harness
grat - wept / cried
gree - prize
greet - weep
grippit - mean
grozet - gooseberry
gropsy - glutton
guddle - mess / mangle
gude - god
gudeman - Good man
guid - good
guidman - master of the house

guid-willie waught – cup of kindness / goodwill drink
gully - large knife
gumlie - muddy
gumption - commonsense
gurlie - rough
gut-scraper - fiddler
gyte - insane / mad

H

ha' - Hall
habber - stutter
haddie - Haddock (fish)
haddin - piossesion
hadna - had not
hae - have
haerst - harvest
haffet - lock of hair
hafflins - halfway
hag - moss
hain - spare
hald - property / hold
hale - fit / hearty
hallow mass - all Saints day
hame - home
han - hand
hand-wal'd - hand picked

hankers - desires
hap - wrap
haply - perhaps / by any chance
harigals - entrails
harkit - listened
hash - oaf / idiot
haster - perplex
haud - hold
hauffet - temple
haugh - low lying meadow by a river
haughs - hollows
haurl - drag
havins - manners
hear'st - do you hear
hee - call
heeze - raise
hen-shin'd - bow-legged
here awa - here about / near
heugh - crag
hinderlets - hind parts
hindmost - last
hing - hang
hinny - honey
hirplin - limping
hizzie - hussy / slag
hoar - frost
hoary - greyish white / silvery

hoast - cough
hool - the husk
hornie - devil
houlet - owl
housal - household
hov'd - swollen
howdie - midwife
howe - hollow / glen
howk - dig
hunkers - haunches
hurdies - buttocks
hure - whore
hurl - throw / crash

I

Icker - ear of corn
ier-oe - great grandchild
ilk - each
ilka - every
ill-deedy - mischievous
ill-willy - ill-natured
ingle - fireplace
ingle-gleede - blazing fireside
ingle-lowe - fire light
intermix'd - intermixed
inviolate's - untouched
ither - other

izles - embers

J

Jad - old horse
jag - pin prick
jauk - daily
jaup - splash
jaw - insolent talk
jawpish - tricky
jimplly - neatly
jinglan - jingling
jink - dodge
jo - sweetheart / love
jockey-coat - overcoat
jocteleg - clasp knife
jouk - dodge
jow - swing
jumpit - jumped

K

kae - jackdaw (bird)
kail - cabbage
kail-whittle - cabbage knife
kail-yard - cabbage patch
kain - rents in kind
kame - comb

katy-handit - left handed
kebars - rafters
kebbuck - cheese
keek - peep / look
keekin' glass - mirror
keel - chalk
Keen - sharp / eager
keepit - kept
kelpies - water spirits
ken - know
kens - knows
ken't - knew
kenspeckle - easily recognized
ket - fleece
kiaugh - anxiety / worry
kin - relatives / family members
kinch - noose
kindred - family
kintra - country
kirk - church
kirn - harvest supper
kirsen - chisten
kiss caups - pledge friendship
kist - chest
kith - acquaintance / friend
kittle (adj) - difficult
Kittle (noun) - tickle

knaggie - nobly
knap - smart blow
knapper - head
knoited - knocked
knowe - hillock / hill
knurl - dwarf
kye - cow
kyte - belly

L

Lac'd - corseted
lade - load
lady-landers - ladybird
laggen - bottom of a dish
laigh - low
laiglen - milking pail / bucket
lairing - sinking
laith - loath / hate
lallan - lowland
lammas - August 1st / harvest
lammie - lamb
landlowper - vagabond / tramp
lane - lone
lang - long
lang syne - long ago
langsum - tedious / boring
lantron - lantern / light

laughan - laughing
laun - land
lave - remainder / rest of
laverock - skylark (bird)
law - hill
lawin - bill
lea' - leave
leal - loyal
lear - learning
lee-lang - live long
leesome - pleasant
leeve - live
leeze - bless
leister - spear
len' - lend
leugh - laugh
leuk - look
libbet - gelded / castrated
lightsome - carefree
limmer - mistress
linket - skipped
linn - waterfall
lint - flax / linseed plant
lippen - trust
loan - lane
loof - palm
loon / loun - lad / roguish boy

loot - allow
loup / lowp - leap / jump
lov'd - loved
lov'st - loves
lowe - flame
lowse - loose
luckie - old woman
luesom - lovely
lug - ear
lugget - having ears
luggie - two handled cup
lum - chimney
luntin - smoking
lume - loom
lure - rather
lurve - love
lyart - grey / withered / old
lye - lie

M

mae - more
Mahoun - Devil
maik - equal
mair - more
maist - most
maister - master
mak - make

mak'sna - matters not
mantie - gown
mang - among
manna - food from God
manteel - mantle
mantling - foaming
maskin pat - tea pot
maught - might
maukin - hare
maun - must
maunna - must not
maut - malt
mavis - thrush / bird
mere / meare - mare / female horse
meikle - large
mein - look / demeanour
melder - milling period
men' - mend
mense - sense / tact
menseless - senseless
menzie - follower
merk - old Scottish coin
mess John - church minister
middin - dunghill / scrapheap
middlins - moderately
milkin' shiel - milking parlour
mim - meek

mim mou'd - gently spoken
min' - remember
mind - bear in mind
mindna - forget
Minnie - mother
mirk - gloom
misca' - abuse
mishanter - mishap / accident
mislear'd - unmannerly / rude
mislippen - disappoint
mismarrow - mismatch
mistaen - mistaken
mith - might
mither - mother
moch - moist
monie - many
mony - many
moolin - crumb
mools - dust
moop - nibble
moosty - mouldy
mottle - dusty
mou' - mouth
moubit - mouthful
moudiwort - mole
muckle - great
muir - moor

mumpit - stupid
musing - thinking
muslin - kail- thin broth (soup)
mutchkin - English pint
mysel - myself

N

na' - not
nack - trick
nae - no
naebody - nobody
naething - nothing
naig - pony
naither - neither
nane - none
nappy - ale / beer
nar - near
nay - no / or rather
neebor - neighbor
needfu' - needful
needna - need not
negleck - neglect
neist - next
neth - below
neuk - corner
newlins - very lately
nicht - night

nick - small cut
nicket - cheated
niest - next
nieve - fist
niffer - exchange
nit - nut
nocht - nought
noddle - brain
norlan - northland
notour - notorious
nourice - nurse
nowte - cattle
nowther - neither

O

o'boot - gratis / free
ocht - aught
ochtlins - in the least
o'erhung - overhung
o'erlay - smock /dress
o'erword - chorus
onie - any
or - before
orra - extra
o't - of it
oughtlins - in the same degree
ouk - week

ourie - shivery
oursels - ourselves
out - owre- above
owre - over
owsen - oxen
owther - either
owthor - author
oxter - armpit

P

pack - intimate
paction - agreement
paidle (noun) - puddle
paidle (verb) - dawdle
painch - paunch / large belly paitrick- partridge (bird)
panfu' - panful
pang - cram
parishen - parish
parridge - porridge
parritch - porridge
pash - head
pat - pot
pattle - plough staff / stick
paughty - proud
pawkie - cunning
pechan - stomach

pechin - out of breath
peet mow - peat stack
peinge - whine
peltry - trash
penny fee - wages
penny wheep - small beer
pensfu' - conceited
philibeg - kilt
phoebus - Apollo / the sun
phraise - flatter
pickle - small quantity
pimpin - low / mean
pine - pain
pinion - cog / part of a birds wing
pint stowp - pint measure
pit - put
plack - pennies
plackless - penniless
pleugh / plew - plough
plouk - pimple / spot
plover - short billed wading bird
poacher court - Kirk Session
pock - pocket
poind - seized
pooch - pouch
pook - pluck
poortith - poverty

pou - pull
pouk - poke / jab
poupit - church pulpit
pouse - push
poussie - hare / cat
pouther - powder
pow - head
pownie - pony
pree'd - tasted
preen - pin
presses - cupboards
preeve - prove
prent - print
prief - proof
prigging - haggling
prostration - subservience
pu' - pull
pultrous - lecherous
pund - pound
pursie - small purse
pussie - hare
pyke - pick
pyle - grain
pystle - epistle

Q

quaite - quiet

quat - quit / give up
quauk - quake / shake
quey - cow
quine - young woman
quer - choir
quo - quoth / humorous

R

rade - rode
raff - plenty
raffan - hearty
ragweed - ragwort
raible - nonsense
rair - roar
ramfeezl'd - exhausted
ramgunshoch - rugged
rampin' - ragging / angry
ram stam - headlong
randie - riotous
rankling - festering
rantin - going on and on about something
rantin - talking passionately
rape- rope
raploch - home-spun
rarely - quickly
rash - rush
rattle - strike / hit

ratton - rat
raucle - fearless
raught - reached
raw - row
rax - stretch
ream - froth
reave - rob / steal
red / rede - advise
reek - smoke / smell
remead - remedy
reuth - pity
richt - right
rief - thieve
rig - ridge
rigs - ridges
riggin - roof
rin - run
ringle-ey'd - white-eyed
ripp - handful of corn
riskit - cracked
rither - rudder
rive - split
roon - round
roose - reputation
roosty - rusty
roving - walking / wandering
rowth - plenty

rowtin - lowing
rozet - rosin
rugh - rough
rullions - coarse shoes
rummle - stir about
rummlegumption - common sense
run - downright
rung - cudgel / weapon
runkle - wrinkle
ruth - sorrow
ryke - reach

S

sab - sob /cry loudly
sae - so
saebins - since it is so
saft - soft
saikless - innocent
sair (verb) - serve
sair (adj) - sore / hard
sairie - sorrowful
sall - shall
sark - shirt
saul - soul
saumont - salmon (fish)
saunt - saint
saut - salt

saw - sow / plant seeds
sax - six
scail - spill
scaith - injury
scantlins - scarcely
scar - scare
sconner - disgust / annoy
scotia - Scotland
scraichin - screaming
scrievin - moving along
scrimpt - short / cut back
sculduggery - fornication
see'd - saw
seelfu - pleasant
seenle - seldom
see'st - do you see
session - court
set - start
shachl't - distorted
shanks - legs
shanna - shall not
shaul - shallow
shavie - trick / prank
shaw - small group of trees
shaw (noun) - woodland
shaw (verb) - show
shawpit - shelled

shaws - stalks
sheugh - ditch
sheuk - shook
shiel - shed
shool - shovel
shoon - shoes
shor'd - threaten
shot - sort
shouldna - should not
shouther - sholder
sic / sik - such
sicker - steady
sidelins - sideways
siller - silver
simmer - summer
sin - since
sirple - sip
skaith- damage / mark
skeigh - skittish / nervous
skellum - rogue / waster
skelpin - rushing
skelvy - layered
skilly - skillful
skinking - watery
skinklin - small
skirl - shriek
sklent - side-look

skrimmish - skirmish / fight
skurrivaig - vagabond / tramp
skyre - shine
skyte - lash
slade - slid
slae - sloe
slaik - lick
slap - gap
slaw - slow
slee - sly
sleekit - sneaky/ smooth / cunning
sloken - slake / quench thirst
sma' - small
smack - kiss
smawly - small
smeddum - powder / malt dust
smeek - smoke
smiddie / smiddy - blacksmith
smirtle - shy smile
smoor - smother
smurr - drizzle
smytrie - group / collection
snakin - sneering
snash - abuse
snaw - snow
sned - cut off
snell - bitter / biting / sharp

sneshin - snuff
snick - latch
snirtle - snigger
snool - snub
snowkit - snuffed
sodger - soldier
sole - sill
sonnet - song
sonsie - pleasant
soom - swim
soor - sour
souk - suck
souple - supple
souter - cobbler / shoe maker
sowp - spoonful
sowther - solder
spae - foretell
spair - spare
spak - spoke
sparely - sparsely
spean - wean / get used to
speat - spate
speel - climb
speet - skewer
speir - ask
spelder - tear apart
spence - parlour

spleuchan - tobacco pouch
splore - frolic / carousal
sprattle - scramble
spreckle - speckled
spirritie - full of spirits
sprush - dressed up
spunk - spirit
spunkie - will o' the wisp
squattle - squat
stab - stake (wooden)
Stacher - stagger
stan' - stand
stane - stone
stang - sting
stank - pool
stap - stop
stapple - stopper
stark - strong
staumrel - silly
staw - sicken
staw - stall
stechin - cramming
steek - stitch
steer - stir
steeve - compact
stell - still
stent - duty

steyest - steepest
stibble - stubble
stickit - stuck
stimpart - quarter measure
stirk - young cow
stoiter - stumble
stotter - stagger
stoun / stown - stolen
stounds - aches
stoure - dust / battle
stown - stolen
stowp - cup
strae - straw
stak - stuck
staike - stroke
stramash - argument / fight
strang - strong
straught - straight
stravaugin - roaming
streekit - stretched
streen - last night
striddle - straddle
studdie - anvil
stumle - stumble
stump - stop / halt
stumpie - stout
sturt - fret / worry

sucker - sugar
sugh - sigh
sumph - blockhead / idiot
sune - soon
suthron - southern
swall'd - swelled
swain - suitor / lover
swally - swallow / drink
swankie - fine fellow
swarf - to swoon
swat - sweat
swatch - sample / little bit
swats - light beer
swee - over
sweer - lazy
swith - get away
swither - hesitate
swoor - swore
syne - since / then

T

tack - lease
tackets - shoe-nails
tae - toe
taen - taken
taigle - hinder
taikle - tackle

tairge - target
taisle - tassel
tak - take
tald - told
tangs - tongs
tap - top
tapetless - thoughtless
tapsalteerie - topsy-turvy
tassie - cup
tauk - talk
tauld - told
teat - small quantity
ted - spread
teen - sorrow / grief
teen - anger
tensum - ten together
tent (noun) - caution
tent (verb) - tend
tentie - careful
tentless - without a care
teugh - tough
teuk - took
thack - thatch
thae - those
thairm - intestines
thankit - thanked
thegither - together

thereanet - about that
thick - inmate
thieveless - forbidding
thiggin - begging
thir - these
thirl - thrill
tho' - although
thocht - thought
thole - endure / suffer
thon - you
thou'se - thou shalt
thowe - thaw
thrang (noun) - a crowd
thrang (verb) - busy
thrapple - throat
thrave - 24 sheaves of corn
thraw - twist
threed - thread
threep - maintain
threesum - three together
threteen - thirteen
thretty - thirsty
thrist - thirst
thrissle - thistle
throu'ther - confused
thumpit - thumped
thurst - thrust

thysel - thyself / yourself
timmer - timber
timmer-tuned - unmusical
tim'rous - fearful
tip / toop - ram (tup) / a sheep
tippenny - small beer
tipper - taiper- teeter
tine - lose
tinkler - tinker / tramp
tint - lost
tippence - two pence
tippenny - two-penny beer
tir - tap
'tis - it is
tither - other
tittle - whisper
tocher - marriage bonds
tod - fox
Tod Lowrie - fox
too fa' - lean-to
toom - empty
tother - other
toun - farmland
towsie/tousie - shaggy
tow - rope
towsing - handling
towmound - twelve-month

toy - cap
tozie - tipsy
traiket - disordered
trashtrie - rubbish
trepan - ensnare
trig - neat
trowth - trust
tryste - appointment
try't - tried
tuffle - ruffle
tulzie - quarrel
tummle - tumble
tummler - cup / glass
tunefu' - tuneful
ture - tore
turkasses - pincers
turn - task
turrs - turfs
twa / tway - two
'twad - would have
twahaund - between two
twal - twelve
twasum - two together
tween - between
tweesh - betwixt / between
twin - sepatate from
twine - twist

tyesday - Tuesday
tyke - dog
tyken - bed linen
tylie - slice of beef
tyest - entice

U

ulzie - oil
unchancy - dangerous
unco - strange / very
undeemous - inconceivable
undocht - silly
uneith - difficult
unfauld - unfold
unfeiry - inactive
unkend - unknown
unkin - unkind
unloosome - unlovely / ugly
unsicker - uncertain
unsneck - unlock
unweeting - unwittingly
uphaud - uphold
upo' - upon
upsides - equal to
upstan't - stood
uptack - understanding
usquabae - whisky

usquebah - whisky

V

van - group
vauntie - proud
vera / verra - very
verdant - green / lush
vernal - springtime
vernal - youthful
vie - compete
virl - ring
vittles - food
vively - clearly
vogie - conceited
vowt - vault / jump

W

wa' - wall
wab - web
wabster - weaver
wad - wager
wad - would
waddin' - wedding
wadna - would not
wae - woe /sorrow
weaness - sadness

waesucks - alas
wair'd - spent
wale - choice
walie - large
wame - belly
wan - won / one
wanchancie - dangerous
wanrestfu' - restless
wanruly - unruly
wanton - promiscuous / frolic deliberate
wanwordy - unworthy
wap - wrap
wappon - weapon
war - were
ware - worn
wark - work
warl' / warld - world
war's gear - worldly possesions
warlock-breef - magic spell
warl'y - worldly
warna - were not
warran - warrant
warse - worse
warsle - wrestle
wart - were it
wast - west
wat - wet

water-fit - mouth of the river
waud - wade
waugh - damp
waught - large dink
wauk - wake
waukrife - sleepless
waukit - calloused
waur - worse
wawlie - handsome
wean - child
weary fa' - plague upon
weason - gullet
wecht - weight
wee - small
weed - clothes
weel - well
weel-hain'd - well-saved
weet - wet
westlin - westerly
wha - who
whae - who
whaizle - wheeze
whalpit - whelped / birthed
whang - slice
whan - when
whar - where
whase - whose

whaup - curlew / bird
whid - fib / move quickly
whigmaleeries - whimsical
whiles - sometimes / at times
whilk - which
whirligigums - useless things
whisht - silence
whitter - measure of liquor
whommilt - turned upside down
whun - basalt / volcanic rock
whunner - rattle
whup - whip
whyles - sometimes
wi' - with
wifie - wife
willyart - awkward
wimple (verb) - wind
wimplin - winding
winch - wench
winna - will not
winnins - earnings / winnings
winnock-bunker – window seat
win's - winds
wise-like - respectable
wiss - wish
written - knowledge
wonner - wonder

woo' - wool
woodie - gallows
wook - weak
wordy - worthy
wrack - vex / annoy
wraith - spirit
wrang - wrong
wran - wren / song bird
wright - carpenter
writer - lawyer
wud - wild
wuddie - rope
wull - will
wure - wore
wursum - putrid
wurtle - writhe / squirm
wyliecoat - flannel vest
wyle - entice / attract
wyss - wise
wyte - blame

Y

Yad - old mare
yaird - yard
yarrow - white flower
yauld - vigorous
yaumer - murmur

ye - you
ye'd - you would
ye'll - you will
yell - barren / empty
yellockin - squalling
yer - your
yersel - yourself
ye'se - ye shall / you shall
yestereen - last evening / night
yett - gate
yill - ale
yince - once
yird - earth
yirdit - buried
yokin - set to
yon - that
yonner - yonder
'yont - beyond
younker - youth
yowe - ewe / a sheep
yowie - lamb / young sheep

ABOUT THE AUTHOR

Alastair Turnbull is a Scotsman and author of Non Fiction books. These books are usually on the subjects of **Scotland**, **Drinking** and **Robert Burns**. These also happen to be three of Alastair's greatest passions in life - after his **wife** and two **daughters**.

Alastair lives in Scotland and has been self-employed for over 15 years in the conference, events and exhibition industry. Working as an Audio-visual technician he has travelled the globe working with a large variety of companies from pharmaceuticals to wind energy specialists, solicitors to potato farmers. If you have no idea what that actually means, just think of him as a corporate "roadie".

Alastair started his writing career with the web site:
www.TheDrinkingMansGuideToScotland.com

This site, which is still very much alive and well, was born after working at endless road shows and events with Scottish drinks producers. There was only so much information he could take in before it started to pour out onto web pages and then onto E-books and magazines. After writing about the great drinks Scotland has to offer, he then started writing about his other two passions: Scotland and Robert Burns.

In his free time Alastair likes to spend time with his family and indulge his three passions. This usually involves him dragging them around yet another Distillery / Brewery / Cider Mill in Scotland, whilst telling them how this relates to Robert Burns work as an excise man.

His family doesn't always enjoy spending time with him.

Christine & Alastair Turnbull

A Little Extra…

*Alastair's wife's maiden name is Christine Burns. Christine's fathers name was **Robert Burns**. He was a farmer from Renfrewshire, (next to Ayrshire).*

ALSO BY ALASTAIR TURNBULL

Robert Burns - Women

Robert Burns - Nature

Robert Burns - Life

Robert Burns - Death

Robert Burns - Scotland

Toasts & Toasting - A Simple Guide to great Toasts, Blessings & Graces

This book is a guide to making a toast, whether it be at a wedding, birthday, graduation, funeral, etc. It also looks at Blessings, Graces, toasting traditions and toasting folklore.

Alastair Turnbull also writes for the web site:

TheDrinkingMansGuideToScotland.com

Printed in Great Britain
by Amazon